The Complete Book on

Everything You Need to Know and Then Some
The First Twelve Years

Jennifer Jones

Illustrated by Barbara Day

ANDANTE PUBLISHING
P.O. Box 507
Redmond, Washington 98073-0507

Dedicated to my children,
Brittany, Christopher, Jason, Amy and Derrick

Acknowledgments

Appreciation is extended to my friends, who have given me inspiration and ideas throughout the years. Special thanks to Barbara Day for her contributions of artistry and creativity.

Many thanks, also, to my family for their continual encouragement, confidence and support. And most importantly, my deepest gratitude to my husband, Frank, who never lets me stop dreaming.

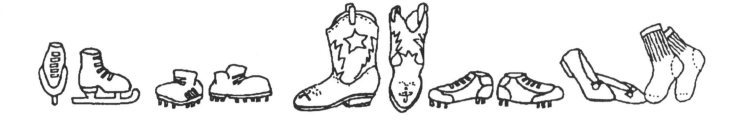

Table of Contents

Introduction

Raising children can be the most wonderful experience of our lives. Yet in today's fast-paced world, as we strive to juggle the many demands placed upon us, we are often too busy and exhausted to enjoy our children the way we would like.

The Complete Book on Kids was created to help parents have happy children and a successful family. This book will especially benefit those whose creativity is not their strongest quality and those whose time and resources may be limited. Each activity is easy and each idea is simple. You will need minimal supplies and absolutely no artistic ability.

Please use this book as a resource and guide. It is hoped that the ideas presented will be explored and expanded to fit the individual needs of your family. It is my sincere desire that this book will make your life just a little bit easier and a little more fun.

The pictures and patterns in this publication have been designed to copy for your *non-commercial* or *home use*. Please remember that all material contained herein is copyrighted and use of this book for personal or monetary gain is prohibited.

FAMILY SAFETY

Basic Information Every Child Must Know

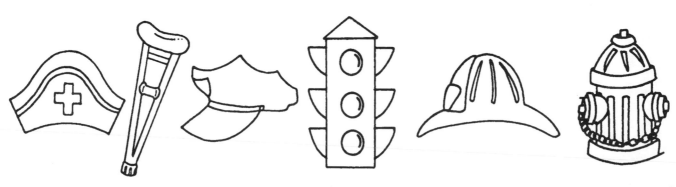

FAMILY SAFETY

Table of Contents

FAMILY SAFETY

Introduction

This chapter was created to help families understand basic safety and to prepare them for possible emergencies.

Often simple precautions can prevent many serious situations from occurring. Knowing what to do in an emergency can make a significant impact on the outcome.

Dwelling on catastrophes and problem situations can often be stressful for children. The ideas presented here, however, are very basic and put forth in a way that is not threatening to a child.

Our children need help to meet the challenge of living safely in our society. They need our guidance. Please take a few minutes and go over this chapter with your children. It could save their lives.

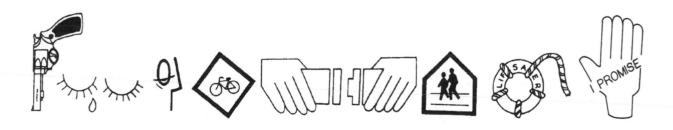

FAMILY SAFETY

I know I should buckle him up, but
we're just going around the block.

I've got some medicine in the cupboard,
I really should have it locked.

I think I'll talk to my husband about
getting rid of his gun.

And one of these days I'll teach my
children how to use 9-1-1.

I should buy electrical outlet covers, but
my chores are not yet done.

I know children shouldn't play in the street,
but they are having so much fun.

When my children get older, I'll talk to
them about drugs and alcohol.

And when I get the money, I'll cover my pool —
a child could easily fall.

There are a lot of things I know I should do
but I seem to procrastinate.

A siren, a screech, a child's cry —
Dear God, am I too late?

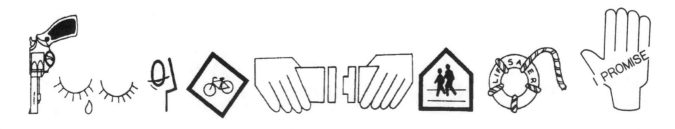

4

Parents' Guide to Safeguarding Your Children

Here are seven important ways you can help your child be safe. Children gain a sense of security when they know you are concerned about their whereabouts and when they know the basic rules of safety.

1. **Watch Your Children**
   - Don't leave them alone in the car, park, store, or other public areas.
   - Know where your children are and whom they are playing with.
   - Always accompany your children to public restrooms.

2. **Teach About Strangers**
   - Teach your children about strangers.
   - Make sure your children know not to get involved with strangers in any way.
   - Teach your children to say no, yell, get away and tell someone if they are bothered by strangers.

3. **Create a Secret Password**
   - Create a secret password that only you and your children know, to help them identify someone who can be trusted.

4. **Establish Family Safety Rules**
   - Teach your children to use the buddy system when away from home.
   - Teach your children all of their family members' first and last names.
   - Make family house and safety rules to be followed in your absence.

5. **Teach and Practice Telephone Use**
   - Teach your children their phone number and how to use the telephone system.
   - Post important phone numbers near the telephone.
   - Make sure your children have a person to contact in case of an emergency.
   - Make sure your children have a backup person to contact in emergencies.
   - Make sure your children know how to call emergency numbers.
   - Teach your children how to answer the telephone in your absence.
   - Teach your children how to handle obscene telephone calls.

6. **Do Not Print Names On Your Children's Clothing**
   - A viewable name puts a stranger on a first-name basis with your child.

7. **Organize Neighbors**
   - Establish safe homes where children can go for help.
   - Make child safety a neighborhood priority by participating in safety programs and projects.

Important Phone Numbers

It is helpful in emergencies to have a list of important phone numbers easily available for children. Make a copy of this list, fill in the phone numbers and keep posted near your phone.

A great activity to have with your children is an "Emergency Night." Gather the family together and review what to do in case of an emergency.

Important Phone Numbers

My Telephone Number _____

My Address _____
_____

Mother _____

Father _____

Grandparents _____

Doctor _____

Hospital _____

Poison Control _____
Other _____

911 Emergency _____

A Child's Guide to

All children should know how to reach 9-1-1 in an emergency. Many lives have been saved because a young child could dial this number. Take a minute and go over the information below with your child. So often in an emergency, it is hard to remember basic information. Copy the form below, fill it out and place it near your phone. This information is also valuable for a babysitter in case of an emergency.

9-1-1 is a Special Emergency Telephone Number

When to call 9-1-1:
- To help someone who is seriously hurt.
- If someone is trying to hurt you.
- If you smell smoke, see fire, or see a crime.

How to Make an Emergency Call to 9-1-1

1. **Stay calm.**

2. **Tell the operator what is wrong:**
   "My house is on fire."
   "My dad is hurt."
   "Someone is trying to get into my house."

3. **Tell them your name and address.**
   Name: _____
   Address: _____

4. **Tell them the phone number you are calling from:**
   Phone Number: _____

5. **Do not hang up until you are told to do so.**

Family Emergency Checklist

What is an emergency?

An emergency is a problem that requires action in order to prevent injury or damage. Losing your homework or spilling something on your clothes is a problem, but it is not an emergency. Emergencies are when someone is hurt or if you smell smoke. Discuss types of emergencies.

Emergency Checklist

- Do you have a contact person your child can reach in case of an emergency? Are the name and telephone number listed near the phone? Do you have a backup contact person in case the first one is not home or the line is busy?

- Is there a list of emergency numbers posted near the phone? Does this list include parents' work numbers, police, fire, paramedics (9-1-1), physicians, utility trouble numbers, poison control, others?

- Does your child know what to do when locked out? Is there a spare key?

- Are you prepared for a blackout? Is there a flashlight in a handy place? Does your child know where the fuse box is and do you want them to know how to restore power?

- Does your child know where the water shut-off is in your home? Do they know where the shut-off valves are for the sinks and toilets?

The fusebox is: _____

The water shut-off is: _____

Flashlights are stored: _____

My contact person is: _____

Child Identification Sheet

It is a good idea to have a child identification sheet for each child in your family.

Copy the Child Identification Sheet on the following page, fill it out and keep in your child's personal file — just in case. (See "Files" in Chapter V, Kids and Their Clutter)

An inkpad for fingerprinting can be purchased at your local variety store.

Child Safety Sheet

When going over safety with your children it is important that the information is reviewed and rehearsed periodically.

To help a child remember safety facts, a "Child Safety Sheet" is included on page 11. Go over the information with your child and let him fill out the form.

When he has completed it and knows the emergency information, reward him. Safety awards are provided on the following pages. Just copy, color, and glue onto space provided on the Safety Sheet.

Safety Contract

Once a child knows the basic rules of safety and your family rules and safety information, you could make a "safety contract" with your children to help them understand the importance of not only knowing the rules, but following them.

You will find "My Safety Contract" on page 13. Copy the form, go over it with your child, have your child fill it out, then sign it. Post it where all can see and review it on occasion. Having the contract posted is especially helpful as a reminder if one of the rules has not been followed.

Child Identification Sheet

Name _____   Date: _____

Birthdate: _____

Age of Child: _____

| Child's Photograph |

Blood Type: _____

SSN#: _____

Nicknames: _____

Child's Handwriting Sample: _____

	Thumb	1st finger	2nd finger	3rd finger	small finger
Left Hand	Thumb	1st finger	2nd finger	3rd finger	small finger
Right Hand	Thumb	1st finger	2nd finger	3rd finger	small finger

Take this form and child to local police department for fingerprinting. They will be happy to help.

Personal Mannerisms:

Medical Problems:

Allergies:

Description of Child:

Identifying Marks:

CHILD SAFETY SHEET

Place Award Here When Sheet is Complete

I know my full name ______________________

I know my telephone # ______________________

I know my address ______________________

I know my parents' names ______________________

I know what to do in case of a fire ______, ________, and __________.

I know what to do if I am on fire ________, ________, and __________.

I know bike safety rules ______________________

I know sidewalk safety rules ______________________

I know gun safety ______________________

I know water safety ______________________

I know how to answer the phone ______________________

I know how to call 9-1-1 ______________________

I know who to call if I need help ______________________

I filled out my Child Identification Sheet ______________________

I always buckle my seatbelt ______________________

Congratulations!

Glue one of these award ribbons on the Child Safety Sheet when you have reviewed all the safety rules and information with your child, and you want to reward him or her for knowing all necessary safety information.

My Safety Contract

I, _____ , promise that:

    Child's Name

1. I will be careful when crossing streets and will obey the crossing signals.

2. I will go directly home from school and let my parents know where I am at all times.

3. I will never take medicine without an adult present.

4. I will never play with matches, electrical sockets, or household cleaners.

5. I will never take anything from a stranger.

6. I will never, never get in a car with a stranger.

7. I will let my parents or an adult know when I see something strange or unusual.

8. I will never play with a gun.

9. I will never play near water.

10. I will obey the basic rules of safety on my bike and on the sidewalk.

Signed: _____ Date: _____

Parent: _____ Date: _____

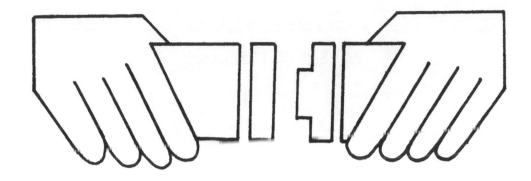

Buckle Up for Life

Many deaths and injuries can be prevented by buckling your child in safely. Yet statistics show that only about 30 percent of children under the age of five are properly restrained.

Use of approved child safety seats can reduce the probability of death in a crash by about 90 percent and severe injury by 70 percent.

Most states have laws regarding child car safety. These guidelines usually are to have children under age two ride in an approved car safety seat; children two years and up to eight must ride in an approved car safety seat or safety belt.

Some children may resist being buckled in. Children who ride in car seats as infants develop the habit and are usually much easier to keep in seats as toddlers. So start early — *always* buckle up your child, then set an example. Wear your own safety belt.

If you cannot afford a car seat, check with your local health department or hospital for rental sites.

Sidewalk Safety

Children need to learn the rules of safe outside play when they are learning to walk. Hundreds of children are hit by cars each year.

1. Cross only at the corner.

2. Watch for turning cars.

3. Obey all the safety signs.

4. Never run across the street. WALK!

5. When using a crosswalk, wait for the signal before you cross the street. Make sure you Stop! Look! and Listen! When all is clear, then walk.

Bicycle Safety Rules

When a child gets his first bike, take a few minutes to go over bike safety rules. It could save a life.

1. Keep your bike in good and safe condition.

2. Ride on the right side of the road.

3. Obey all signs.

4. Use hand signals.

5. Yield to pedestrians at crosswalks.

6. Do not weave in and out of traffic.

7. Learn to ride your bicycle in a safe place.

8. Do not ride double on your bicycle.

9. Wear a bike helmet!

  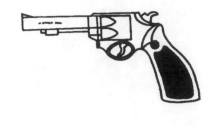

Gun Safety

Gun injuries are increasing at an alarming rate. Children must know that guns are not toys. Guns are not to play with. They can kill.

Here are some guidelines for safety with a gun to go over with your children:

1. If you find a gun, *do not touch it.* If indoors, report it to a parent. If outdoors, report it to the police.

2. Stay away from it. Keep others away from it.

3. Never show it to your playmates.

4. Never, never point a gun at anyone — not even a toy gun, just in fun.

5. And…never let someone point a gun at you!

A note to parents: If you are a gun owner, ALWAYS keep your gun unloaded and in a locked cabinet. A trigger lock should also be used. These locks are available for about $10.

Poison Safety

Hundreds of children are accidentally poisoned each year by eating or drinking items in the home. There are three things a parent can do to prevent an accidental poisoning:

1. Keep dangerous medicines, cleaners and chemicals locked up or out of reach of small children. (Remember — children can climb.)

2. Teach your child about the danger of ingesting harmful substances.

3. Mark dangerous liquids. Always keep syrup of ipecac available. Have the poison control number posted near your phone, and watch children carefully.

16

Fire Safety

Fire prevention is an important part of child safety. Children should be taught how to prevent a fire and what to do in case of a fire.

Go over these steps with your child. Make a map of your house on the grid provided and have a plan for an emergency exit.

1. Never play with matches.
2. Never cook without an adult.
3. Never play with wires or electrical outlets.

If you ever have fire on you: **1. STOP**

                                      2. DROP

                                      3. ROLL

If you are in a building with a fire:

1. Quickly walk out the nearest exit.
   If there is too much smoke, crawl to the nearest exit.

2. Call the Fire Department.

What To Do In A Fire

Spend an evening discussing fire prevention. Then plan with your family what to do and where to go in the event of a fire.

Use the grid below to map out your house, particulary noting doors and windows. Use the ideas below to ensure safer behavior in case of a fire.

1. Choose a place. Have a pre-arranged family meeting place where everyone should assemble.

2. Know two ways out of every room, especially bedrooms. Make sure children can unlock doors and windows and have a way to get down from second story windows.

3. Get out fast! Walk quickly; if it's smoky, crawl fast. Go to the family meeting place.

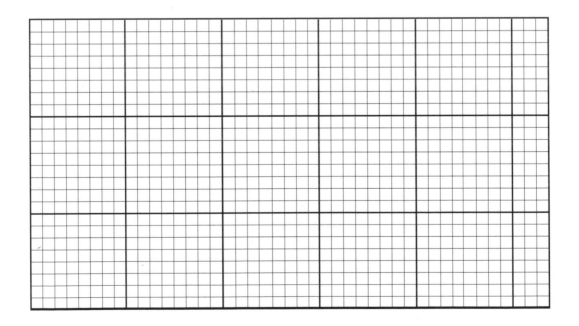

Water Safety

Hundreds of children drown each year in the United States. All children should learn to swim. It is also important that children know basic water safety rules.

1. Learn to swim.

2. If you do not know how to swim, do not go near water without an adult.

3. If you know how to swim, always swim with a friend.

4. Choose a safe spot for swimming.

5. Test how deep the water is before you jump in.

6. Always follow pool safety rules.

7. Never dunk anyone under water.

Safety With Animals

Some children are fascinated with animals; others are extremely scared. It is a good idea to teach children basic safety rules to help them understand proper treatment of animals.

1. Never tease or hurt an animal. Never use an animal to scare another person.

2. Don't bother animals when they are eating or sleeping.

3. Don't bother mothers when they are alone with their babies.

4. Always ask permission before handling someone else's pet.

5. Don't stick fingers in cages.

6. Leave wildlife alone. A wild animal that appears friendly may be sick.

7. Move slowly and talk softly around unknown animals. You never want to startle an animal.

8. Never attempt to move an injured animal. Ask an adult to call Animal Control Services so that an injured animal can be properly helped.

Drug and Alcohol Prevention

Alcohol and other drugs are an ever-increasing threat in our society. The availability of drugs to our children is astonishing.

There are many things parents can do to help their children understand the importance of not taking drugs.

- Talk with your child. Don't lecture. Listen to his or her experiences.

- Review newspaper articles and show children examples of what happens to those who take drugs.

- Make sure there are drug-free alternatives for young people.

- Get involved in drug prevention groups found through the PTA, Boy and Girl Scouts, community centers, and religious groups. If there is not one available, start a program of your own through parent workshops, peer counseling, neighborhood groups, or PTA activity.

- Check at your local library for books and articles concerning drug prevention.

- Police stations often have literature they can provide free of charge.

- Contact any drug prevention program for more information and literature. Some resources are listed on the following page.

21

Drug and Alcohol Prevention Resources

National Clearinghouse for Alcohol and Drug Information (NCADI)
PO Box 2345
Rockville, MD 20852
310-468-2600

American Council for Drug Education (ACDE)
204 Monroe St.
Rockville, MD 20850
301-294-0600

National Federation of Parents for Drug-Free Youth (NFP)
Communication Center
1423 N. Jefferson
Springfield, MO 65802
417-836-3709

Parents Resource Institute for Drug Education (PRIDE)
The Hunt Building
Suite 210
50 Hunt Plaza
Atlanta, GA 30303
800-241-9746

D.A.R.E. America, Inc.
P. O. Box 2767
Culver City, CA 90231-2767

National Crime Prevention Council (NCPC)
1700 K Street, NW
Second Floor
Washington, DC 20006
202-466-NCPC

The National PTA
700 Rush St.
Chicago, IL 60611
312-787-0977

Just Say No Foundation (JSN)
1777 N. California Blvd.
Suite 200
Walnut Creek, CA 94596
800-258-2766
(in CA 415-939-6666)

National Drug Information Center of Families in Action (FIA)
2296 Henderson Mill Road
Suite 204
Atlanta, GA 30345
404-934-6364

The Chemical People
WQED
4802 Fifth Avenue
Pittsburg, PA 15213

Finding a Good Babysitter

Parents need to feel comfortable with whomever they have chosen to take care of their children. Finding a good babysitter can be a difficult and painstaking ordeal. Following are a few suggestions to help you choose the right sitter for your family.

1. Ask around. Neighbors, church members, or daycare providers are great resources for providing references.

2. Invite the prospective sitter over to see how he or she interacts with your children.

3. Provide the sitter with information. Let her know your family rules and guidelines concerning bedtime, telephone usage, and having friends over.

4. Determine pay schedule in advance to avoid problems.

5. Ask questions. Does the sitter know first aid? The Heimlich Maneuver? How much experience does he or she have?

Safety While Babysitting

1. Always get your parents' permission before accepting any babysitting job.

2. Always provide your parents with the family's name, address and phone number and the time you can be expected home.

3. Always have a ride to and from your babysitting job.

4. Know the people you are sitting for; require references.

5. Have an emergency telephone list, complete with the family's name and address.

6. Know where you can reach the parents, and ask for another name and telephone number to call in an emergency.

7. Answer telephone calls and take messages, but never tell a caller you are babysitting.

8. Keep windows, doors, and gates locked.

9. Know where to find a flashlight and a first aid kit.

10. Never let a stranger in the house. If they persist, call the police.

11. Watch the children closely — stay with them at all times. Do not let them play with matches, knives, or other sharp or dangerous objects.

12. Take a first aid class and learn CPR. Learn how to do the Heimlich Maneuver. It could save a child's life.

Choosing Daycare

With many children spending much of their time in daycare, it is becoming increasingly important to screen the people you want your children to be with. Consider the values and behaviors that are being taught as well as the educational instruction. Below are some guidelines to help you in choosing your daycare or babysitter.

In any childcare situation, it is a good idea to drop in unannounced occasionally. Talk with your child daily about how things are going. Investigate problems and compare notes with other children. Believe your child if he feels uncomfortable or demonstrates unusual behavior.

1. Find out as much as you can about the program's reputation and whether there have been any past complaints. Is it licensed or regulated in any way?

2. Learn about the teachers and caregivers. What are their professional qualifications? Are background checks run before they are hired?

3. Make sure you have the right to visit anytime, without an appointment.

4. Find out how children relate to the staff. Are they happy and involved, or do they pull away from staff members?

5. Ask about the philosophy of discipline.

6. Make sure there is parent involvement, such as group meetings and parent conferences.

7. Never give the organization blanket permission to take your child off the premises.

8. Prohibit, in writing, the release of your child to anyone without your authorization.

Preventing Child Sexual Abuse

The most important aspect of child sexual abuse prevention is for parents to have an open line of communication with their children.

1. Talk and listen to your child. Be involved in their activities. Know the people they associate with. Encourage your child to share and discuss problems or concerns with you.

2. Make sure your children know that they have control over their bodies. They have the right to say no to anyone who might hurt them.

3. Let your children know that there are some adults who are not good, who may try to hurt them. They may try to get them to do something that is not right. They may call it a secret, they may offer a special treat, or even threaten a child.

4. Most adults are nice and will help children. Children must know that they can always tell their mom or dad, grandma, teacher, or an adult they trust, if someone tries to hurt them.

Symptoms of Sexual Abuse

Some children may be too frightened to discuss sexual abuse. Usually, however, there are physical symptoms that may occur which could signify molestation.

1. Fear of a person, or an intense dislike at being left with someone.

2. Torn or stained underclothing.

3. Extreme changes in behavior.

4. Nightmares, disturbed sleep patterns.

5. Unusual interest in or knowledge of sexual matters, or expressing affection in ways inappropriate for a child of that age.

6. Vaginal or rectal bleeding, pain, itching, swollen genitals, venereal disease, or vaginal infections.

7. Regression to more infantile behavior (i.e., bedwetting or excessive crying).

8. Other behavioral signals: aggressive or disruptive behavior; withdrawal; failing in school; or delinquent behavior.

9. Unusual behavior with dolls or stuffed animals of a sexual nature.

Additional Safety Helps

For more safety information, there are many resources in your community who would be glad to help. Call and set up a time to go visit your local fire department or police station. Your community Health and Human Services Department has many pamphlets, brochures, and information — usually free of charge. Local hospitals frequently have classes concerning safety — everything from buckling up infants to babysitting classes.

Contact your school PTA to have classes on safety taught in your schools, or get some of your neighbors together and have your own classes.

Your Police Department would be glad to help you set up a neighborhood crime watch.

Check around and see what you can do to protect your family.

Facts

Fact: Falls hurt and kill more kids than any other kind of accident at home.

Fact: The use of alcohol frequently precedes the use of marijuana and other drugs, particularly when alcohol use is begun before or during teen years.

Fact: At least 100,000 children are reported as victims of sexual abuse each year.

Fact: You can reduce the probability of deaths from car accidents by 90% if you buckle your seat belt.

Fact: Hundreds of children die each year in the U.S. because they hurt their heads in bike accidents.

Fabulous Fun for the Whole Family

Table of Contents

Introduction

In the hustle and bustle of our everyday lives, it seems that we don't always take time out to spend it with those we love the most.

The ideas in this chapter are designed for families to spend quality time together. They are given to help families have fun while learning and growing closer to one another.

These ideas require little planning or money, just a family eager to enjoy one another's company.

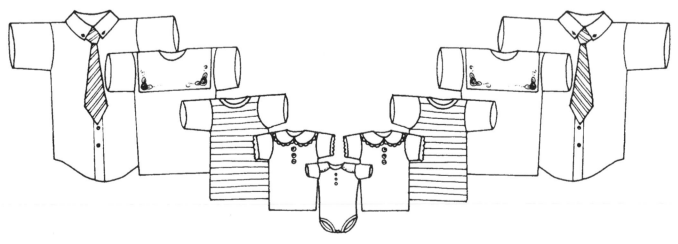

FAMILY FUN

My family likes to laugh and play
    But lots of times we fight.
Sometimes we stay up late and talk
    'Til the middle of the night.

My family often works together
    When we have a job to do.
We pull the weeds and wash the car
    To name just a few.

We don't always get along,
    It is not always fun.
But it usually ends up okay
    When all the work is done.

Dad is really busy,
    He has a lot to do.
But he finds time to play with me
    When his work is through.

Sometimes I get mad at Mom,
    She gets mad at me, too.
But she is good at listening
    When I'm feeling blue.

We try so hard to cooperate
    It's very hard to share.
But even when we get in trouble
    We know our parents care.

The boys in my family like to tease,
    and the little ones always whine.
I don't mind too much, you see
    Because this family's mine.

My family isn't perfect
    As you can plainly see.
They are all sort of crazy
    But they belong to me.

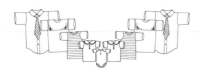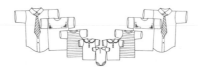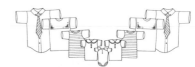

50 Ideas for Kids to Do in the Summer

1 Plant seeds in an egg carton

2 Go to the library

3 Sweep garage

7 Build a club house

4 Pick up empty bottles or cans

5 Plant some berry bushes

6 Take a bus ride

8 Go to the zoo

9 Weed the garden

11 Give your dog a bath

10 Visit Dad's work

12 Start a collection

13 Learn about the stars

14 Make a macaroni necklace

15 Take a treat to a neighbor

16 Plan a surprise for Mom

19 Run through sprinklers

18 Play with water balloons

17 Visit or write to Grandma & Grandpa

23 Mow the lawn

21 Play marbles

20 Have a water fight

24 Visit Mom's work

22 Make a photo book of summer activities

25 Teach your dog a new trick

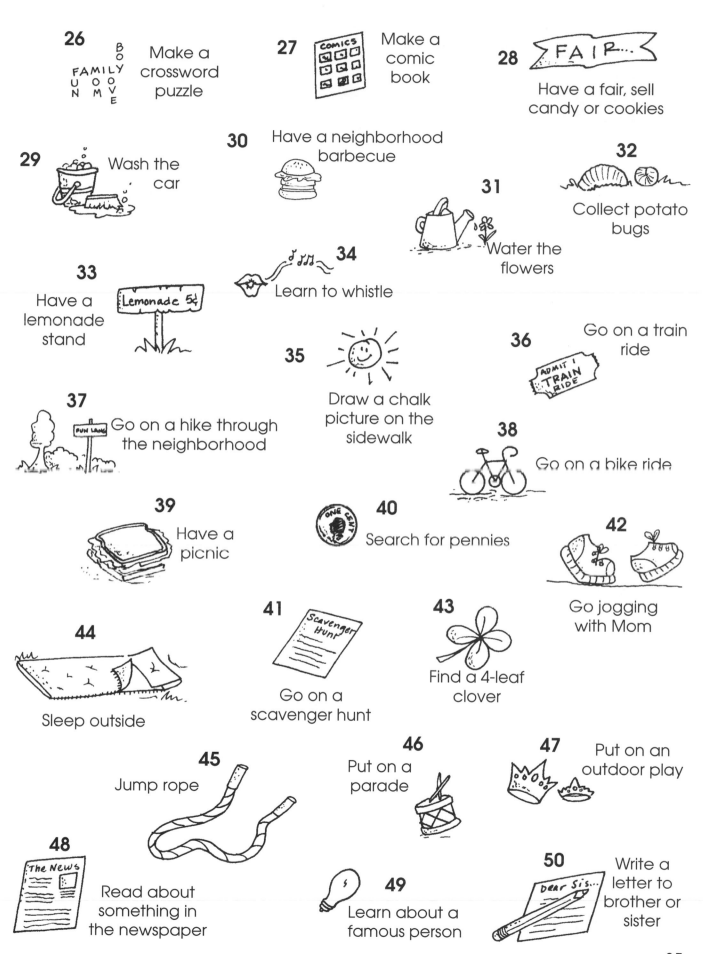

26 Make a crossword puzzle

27 Make a comic book

28 Have a fair, sell candy or cookies

29 Wash the car

30 Have a neighborhood barbecue

31 Water the flowers

32 Collect potato bugs

33 Have a lemonade stand

34 Learn to whistle

35 Draw a chalk picture on the sidewalk

36 Go on a train ride

37 Go on a hike through the neighborhood

38 Go on a bike ride

39 Have a picnic

40 Search for pennies

41 Go on a scavenger hunt

42 Go jogging with Mom

43 Find a 4-leaf clover

44 Sleep outside

45 Jump rope

46 Put on a parade

47 Put on an outdoor play

48 Read about something in the newspaper

49 Learn about a famous person

50 Write a letter to brother or sister

50 Ideas for Kids to Do in the Winter

1 Read a good book

2 Have a family restaurant

3 Go sledding

4 Have an indoor picnic

5 Learn some magic tricks

6 Start making Christmas gifts

8 Learn to play harmonica

7 Build a snowman

9 Feed birds dry bread

10 Grow an indoor garden

12 Plan a summer vacation

11 Paint some rocks

13 Put a model together

14 Make a soap snowman

15 Play dress-up

17 Go to a museum

18 Visit a pet store

19 Memorize a poem

16 Collect old blankets to donate to the zoo

20 Clean under your bed

22 Write letters

21 Sharpen all pencils

23 Make a family newspaper

24 Sort out your toy box

25 Invite friends to lunch

26 Bake cookies

27 Do some puzzles

28 Make Christmas ornaments

29 Write some poetry

30 Learn where countries are on the globe or map

31 Visit a lonely neighbor

Use stencils for a picture **32**

33 Write in a diary or journal

34 Learn how to tie knots

38 Make a spook alley

35 Clean out your drawers

36 Plan a summer vacation

37 Do face painting

39 Make glitter snowflakes

41 Teach a small child ABCs

40 Start a child's exercise program

42 Make some goals

My Goals are...

43 Make snow angels

44 Have a fire drill

45 Comb your dog or cat

46 Have a mini pilgrim feast

48 Play a board game

Make a collage out of magazine pictures

47

49 Make a treasure hunt

51 Plan your Halloween costume

50 Put on a puppet show

30 Fun Family Activities

1. Treasure Box

In September, before school starts, make a family treasure box. Bury the box filled with photographs, pictures, outline of hands, shoe size and a list of goals. Unbury your treasure box the next fall and see how you have done!

2. Story Lesson

Whenever a child has a need to learn an important lesson, find a story dealing with that situation. Have the child help create a play or puppet show to demonstrate that situation.

3. Family T-Shirts

Buy matching T-shirts for each family member. Paint a family logo on each one. This is a great way to keep track of everyone on vacation. (Do not put child's name on shirt.)

4. Family Visors or Hats

Matching visors or hats are another way to have family unity. Plastic visors, painter's hats or plain baseball caps are inexpensive and can be found in a craft store. Decorate or paint a family logo on top.

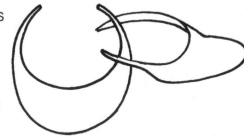

5. Start a Collection

Here is a fun project for families. Decide what you want to collect and have all family members help. Some ideas: books, key chains, postcards, cookie cutters, puppets, stamps, or insects — or pick a theme, such as hearts, frogs, skies, or clouds.

6. Sound Scavenger Hunt

Write a list of sounds in your neighborhood. Grab a tape recorder and see how many sounds you can get in 30 minutes.

7. Sponsor a Neighborhood Potluck

Invite each neighbor to bring something to eat. Spread out blankets and enjoy. This is a great way to get to know your neighbors. (See invitation pattern on next page.)

8. Family Sport Events

Go to a park and play a game (baseball, soccer, tennis, or whatever your family loves). Invite another family, too, then have a picnic.

30 Fun Family Activities (cont'd.)

Here's a unique idea for invitations to your Neighborhood Get-Together

- Fold top in first, then bottom, inside hand, then hook thumbs to outside hand.

- Color.

- Print message on inside with time, date, and place.

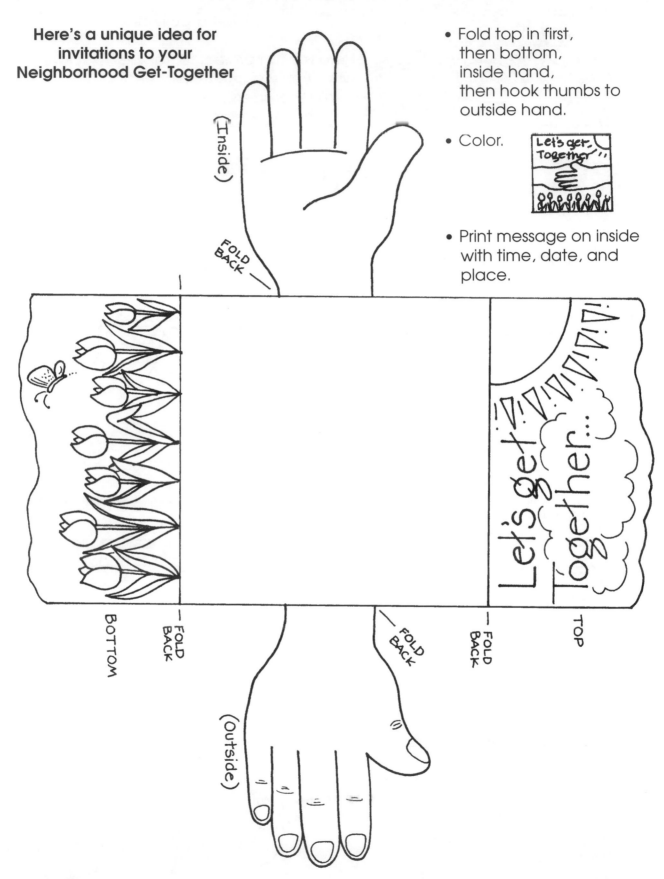

(Inside)

FOLD BACK

BOTTOM

FOLD BACK

FOLD BACK

FOLD BACK

TOP

Let's get Together...

(Outside)

30 Fun Family Activities (cont'd.)

9. Memory Night

If you want to put together baby books, scrapbooks, or personal histories, devote one evening a month to a family member. Have everyone remember everything they can about that person. Tape record or write the session. This is a great self-esteem booster for each child and helps your family to catch up on keeping memories.

10. Family Field Trips

- Dairy
- Newspapers
- Restaurants
- Police Station
- Greenhouse
- Television Stations
- Post Office
- Fire Stations
- Florist Shop
- Car Wash
- Grocery Store
- Farm

It's fun to do things together with your family. Once a month plan a family field trip. There are many places in your community which you can visit free of cost. Look for other activities in your community.

11. Family Garden

Have each family member plant a row of vegetables. They then are responsibile for weeding that row through the summer. Then have a special dinner using all vegetables to celebrate all your hard work.

1. Copy pages of garden markers onto cardstock.
2. Have children color.
3. Laminate or apply clear plastic shelf paper to both sides.
4. Attach Popsicle® sticks to back and mark rows of veggies, fruits and flowers.

CAULIFLOWER

41

CAULIFLOWER

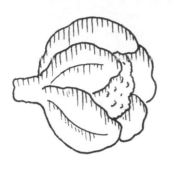

BEANS

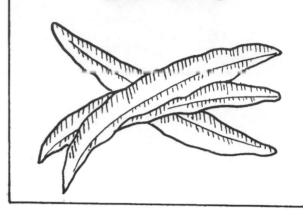

STRAWBERRIES

PUMPKIN

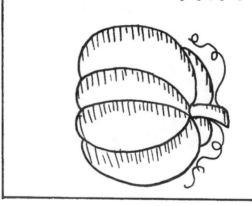

BROCCOLI

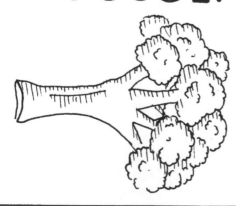

CUCUMBER

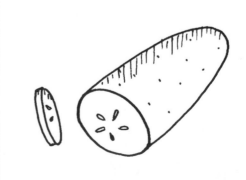

RADISHES

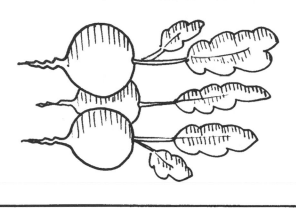

ONIONS

POTATOES

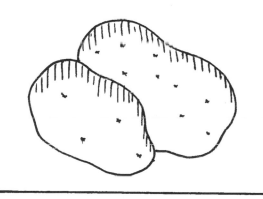

PEAS

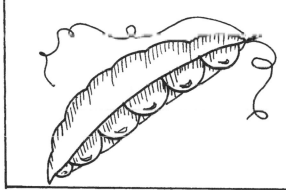

TOMATOES

ASPARAGUS

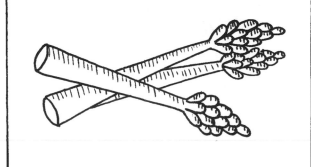

CARROTS

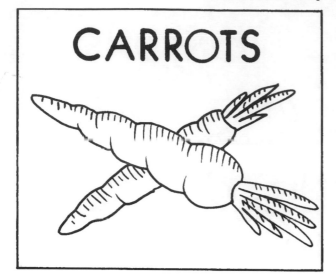

BEETS

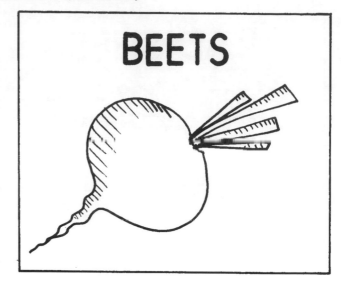

LETTUCE

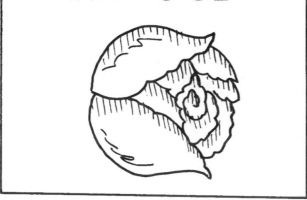

SQUASH

CABBAGE

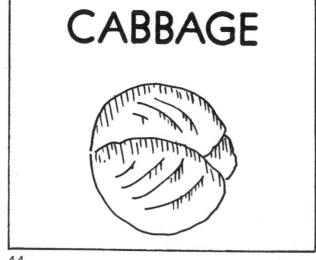

CORN

30 Fun Family Activities (cont'd.)

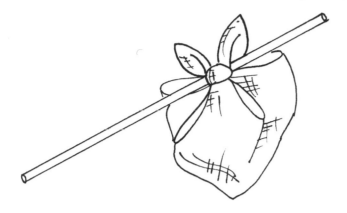

12. Morning Hike

Make this hobo pack for a family morning hike. Get up early and go for a little hike (even if it is around the block). Then, watch the sun rise or have breakfast outside if the weather is nice.

13. Family Sleep-Out

Either in the outside warmth of summer or by your fire on a cold winter night, a family sleep-out is a great adventure. You don't have to do much planning and organizing, but you get great rewards. Roast marshmallows or make s'mores for an extra treat.

14. Remember the Past

Pick an older person in your neighborhood. Invite them to your home for an evening to share their experiences. Have a special treat prepared. A special mug, filled with hot chocolate mix, marshmallows, mints, and candies will be a special memory.

15. Foreign Night

Pick a country your family has an interest in. Make a special dinner from that country. Learn about the customs, clothing, and history of that country.

16. Family Stationery

Create your own family stationery. Design cards and thank you notes together. Then encourage children to keep in touch with relatives and friends.

1. Have each family member draw a picture. Pick a theme: favorite animal, hand prints, pictures of themselves, or a favorite toy.

2. Reduce down at a copy shop, then add a straight border to go along the bottom of cards or papers.

3. Make several copies of the completed stationery. Seal with stickers or stamps. You can have rubber stamps made of pictures and then use them to decorate envelopes or postcards.

17. Family Interviews

About once a month, have a parent interview each child. This is a great opportunity for parents to really be in touch with each child. This is also a great experience for children. They understand that you are concerned and that they have an opportunity to discuss any problems they might have in privacy.

To go one step further, keep a notebook of questions asked during each interview and write responses. This is a great way to start a family history and see how each child progresses. It also helps with any follow-through you might need.

Some ideas for family interview questions.
1. How do you feel about school? Scouts? Friends? Church?

2. What is the most important thing about yourself?

3. What is your favorite thing about our family?

4. How could our family be better?

30 Fun Family Activities (cont'd.)

18. Scavenger Hunt

Divide family into equal teams. Set a time limit. The team which finds the most items wins.

Ideas: a white stone, a yellow flower, an ant, a clover, a leaf, a pinecone, a popsicle stick, a round object, or a feather.

19. Soap Carving Night

Using dull table knives or a stick, carve designs into a bar of soap. Use them for nice smelling decorations in the bathroom or let kids use them in the tub.

20. Obstacle Course

Set up a course which calls for a variety of skills. Vary course for differing ages. Time each child and let them try to beat their own score.

Ideas: run to a tree, hop 5 times, throw a ball into a bucket, skip around house, jump in a tire, do a somersault, or 5 jumping jacks.

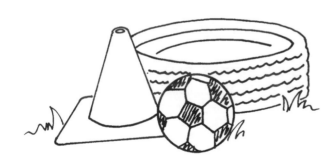

21. Family Flag

Make a flag just for your family. Create a symbol or use your name to design a flag with special meaning for your family. This is a great gift for relatives.

30 Fun Family Activities (cont'd.)

22. Family Drive-In

Set up room like a theater. Have someone be the waiter and take orders for hot dogs and popcorn. Then watch home videos. Use popcorn container found in Classy Container section and fill with popcorn, licorice, and canned drink for each member.

23. Feed the Birds

Make bird seed cookies. Add bird seed to bacon grease. Let it get firm. Cut bread into different shapes and spread birdseed mixture on bread. Tie bird cookies to a tree with string.

String together popcorn, cranberries, fig cookies and bread to make a long garland. Hang around trees for a yummy treat for birds.

24. Letters of Love

Have each person write a letter to the other family members about special things that person has done and qualities that person possesses. They can be shared or placed in a special box to be opened on their birthday.

25. Indoor Magic Garden

Pineapple:

Plant pineapple top in potting soil in a clay or plastic pot. Position plant near top of pot. Water regularly. A pineapple tree will begin to grow.

Lentils:

Spread dried lentils on a plate. Cover with water and set on a window sill. In a few days you'll have shoots.

Carrot, Beet, and Turnip:

Slice top off carrot or other vegetable. Stand in saucer with $1/2$ inch of water. In a week you'll see shoots coming up.

Grass:

Sprinkle a wet sponge with grass seeds and soil. Keep wet and watch your lawn grow.

Orange, Date, and Grapefruit Seeds:

Soak seeds overnight. Plant $1/2$ inch deep in potting soil. Water daily.   A little green plant will soon appear.

Avocado:

Place toothpicks in side of avocado to suspend in a glass. Fill glass with water to cover tip.

26. Family Exercise Program

Get everyone up 15 minutes early and exercise together or go for a brisk walk. Then follow up with a nutritious breakfast. This is a great habit for children and parents to get into. *A complete physical is recommended before any exercise program is started.*

3 areas of focus: **1**. Aerobics, **2**. Strength, and **3**. Stretching.

1. Aerobics
For best result, you should do some kind of aerobics three times weekly for at least 20 minutes each day. Aerobic exercise includes jogging, swimming, walking, biking, jumping rope, or aerobic dance.

2. Strength
Push-ups, pull-ups, sit-ups, weight-lifting.

3. Stretching

Chart Suggestions

- Copy chart on the following page, one chart for each person.

- Laminate or cover with clear contact paper to reuse.

- Use grease pencil or stickers to mark off progress.

One Week Chart

Name	Push ups	Sit ups	1 mile jog	etc...
Days of the week				

Two Week Chart

Name	Monday	Tuesday	Wednesday	etc..
5 min Jump rope				
5 mile bike ride				
etc..				

30 Fun Family Activities (cont'd.)

27. Family Projects

Put together scrapbooks, refinish furniture, do a service project for a neighbor, or make a family flag. Even cleaning the garage will be more fun if it is done together. Children will take more pride in their belongings when they participate in taking care of them.

28. Shower Curtain

Create a family shower curtain. Use the following ideas or create your own.

1. Purchase a full- or queen-size sheet.
2. Using fabric paints, make footprints, handprints, or sponge stamp designs.
3. Splatter paint on with paint brush.
4. Use eyelet maker tool to make holes.
5. Place plastic shower curtain on inside and have designed curtain on outside.

29. Cookie Decorating Contest

Make a batch of sugar cookies and let each child decorate several. Have them pick their favorite one. Of course, everyone is a winner. Prizes go to most creative, prettiest, wildest, or brightest.

30. Talent Show

Pick a special night for a family talent show. Let children prepare for a week or so. They can learn a song, draw a picture, bake a treat, recite a poem, perform and dance, or learn to juggle. Talk about other talents children may have, including a talent for listening, a talent for keeping room organized, a talent for sharing, a talent for sports, or sewing.

Creative Kids

Encouraging Creativity in Kids

Creative Kids

Table of Contents

Creative Kids

Introduction

Encouraging creativity is an important element of child-rearing. Allowing children to express their ideas in an imaginative way reaffirms their uniqueness and builds their self-esteem. This chapter offers parents numerous ways to help their children grow creatively.

The first of the four sections in this chapter, **Dazzling Displays**, gives several ideas for children to utilize their creations — everything from flannel boards to puppet theaters.

The second section, **Classy Containers**, is a collection of ten containers. Most are extremely simple for children to make and decorate. Others are for parents to make and their children to enjoy.

Clever Costumes is full of simple and basic costumes for creative play. Each costume idea is given as a basis to expand and create your own original ideas.

Quick Crafts is the last section in this chapter. These are easy projects children can make with little or no help.

Creative Kids

Mom can you get me
a box of new crayons?
I need a red pencil
and some new rubber bands.

I'll need a big box
and, of course, lots of glue.
I have to have yarn,
both yellow and blue.

I must have some scissors
and some ice pop sticks.
Paste, paint and pens,
and several toothpicks.

I need a ruler,
and a long yardstick.
Some paper and glitter,
oh Mom, please be quick.

I need a green marker,
oh Mom, one more thing —
I almost forgot
I needed some string.

I think now I'm ready
But wait! Goodness sake!
I've got all my stuff,
but Mom, what should I make?

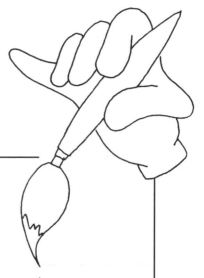

Encouraging Creativity

It is important, as parents, that we develop the ability to allow creativity in our children. While we strive to help our children grow and develop, we must also allow them the opportunity to express themselves and their individuality. Below is a list of ten ideas parents can use to help their children develop creativity and self-esteem.

1. Trust in your children so they can trust in themselves.
2. Provide openness, flexibility, and a variety of choices.
3. Encourage fun, fantasy, and enjoyment.
4. Discourage competition while encouraging cooperation.
5. Create feelings of belonging and security.
6. Encourage problem-solving approaches and communication.
7. Value individuality, difference, uniqueness.
8. Eliminate censorship.
9. Encourage a child to experiment and try.
10. Genuinely appreciate and praise a child's creativity.

50 Creative Ways a Child Can Express Ideas

1. A Letter
2. A Lesson
3. Advertisement
4. Annotated Bibliography
5. Art Gallery
6. Block Picture Story
7. Chart
8. Choral Reading
9. Collage
10. Collection
11. Comic Strip
12. Crossword Puzzle
13. Debate
14. Demonstration
15. Diorama
16. Display
17. Editorial
18. Essay
19. Experiment
20. Fact File
21. Fairy Tale
22. Family Tree
23. Filmstrip
24. Flip Book
25. Game

26. Graph
27. Hidden Picture
28. Illustrated Story
29. Labelled Diagram
30. Learning Center
31. Legend
32. Letter to the Editor
33. Map
34. Mobile
35. Model
36. Mural
37. Museum Exhibit
38. Newspaper Story
39. Origami
40. Oral Report
41. Pamphlet
42. Papier Mâché
43. Photo Essay
44. Poem
45. Poster
46. Project Cube
47. Puppet Show
48. Science Fiction Story
49. Sculpture
50. Skit

Adding Dazzle to Their Masterpieces

Dazzling Displays

1. Flannel Boards
2. Chalk Boards
3. Bulletin Boards
4. Cork Boards
5. Hanging Puppet Theater
6. Box Puppet Theater
7. Shoe Box Movie Screen
8. Easy Box Bookshelf

Displaying children's work is an important part of appreciating their masterpieces. A bulletin board is a great way to show off a special art project from school or work well done. You can purchase ready-made bulletin boards at various stores, but they are often fairly expensive. To make your own …

This section gives you eight creative ways for a child to use and display his creativity. Puppet shows are more fun with a puppet theater. Flannel board stories are a great way to teach children, and children can play with a flannel board and figures for hours.

1. Flannel Boards

To make your own flannel board, simply cover one side of a piece of lightweight plywood with flannel. Use spray glue to attach flannel onto front. Glue flannel to back with heavier glue.

2. Chalk Boards

To make your own chalkboard, spray a piece of hardboard with chalkboard paint (available at most hardware stores). When paint dries, paint the child's name or the alphabet across the top. (This is a great way to restore old chalkboards as well.)

3. Bulletin Boards

A bulletin board is a great way to display children's artwork. Cover a piece of cork or hardboard with fabric or wallpaper and hang on wall. If cork is used, then artwork can be pinned up with push pins. If a hardboard is covered with fabric or wallpaper, hang artwork with tape.

4. Cork Boards

Cork boards make great bulletin boards, too. Purchase squares of cork and hang on wall. Make it as big or small as needed.

5. Hanging Puppet Theater

An easy way for all those puppets to perform.

Things You Need:

> 1 spring rod 36" long or to fit door frame
>
> Heavy fabric 30" x 5 ft (denim or canvas)
>
> Scissors
>
> Glue, paint, extra fabric for decorations

1. Sew 1" casing on top of fabric.
2. Cut out a 16" x 8" rectangle at child's chest level, sew around edges.
3. Hem sides and bottom of panel.
4. Decorate as desired.
5. Put spring rod through casing and hang in doorway.

6. Box Puppet Theater

A very simple way to have hours of fun.

1. Cut top and back off a box.

2. Cut a rectangle on center front.

3. If desired, glue a ruffled lace or fabric onto inside of box for added effect.

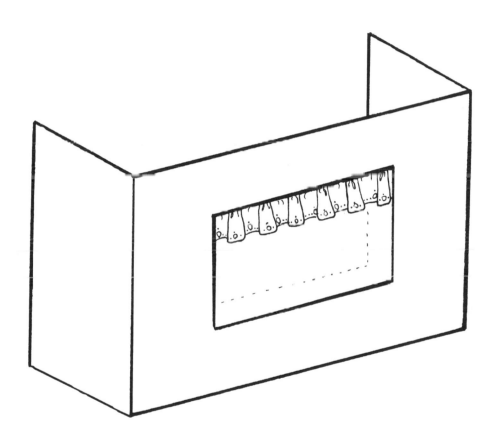

7. Shoe Box Movie Screen

An easy way to create your own movies.

Things You Need:

       Roll of White Paper (freezer paper or shelving paper) 5" wide

       Empty Shoe Box

       Crayons, Markers, Pencils to create your movie

1. Cut 2 slits 5" long on top and bottom of shoe box.
2. Mark off paper in sections about 6" long. Color picture in each section.
3. Re-roll paper, then thread paper from bottom of box, through slits and out top.
4. Pull paper up and watch your movie.

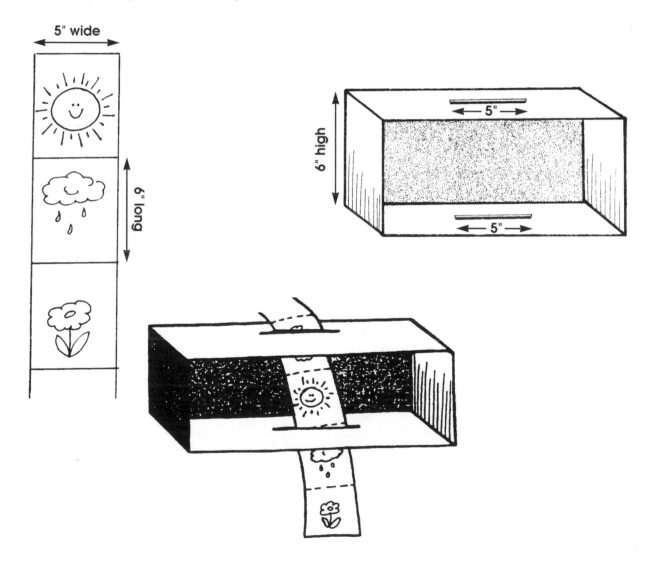

8. Easy Box Bookshelf

Things You Need:

Box (approximately 10" x 10" x 12")
Scissors

1. Cut top off box.
2. Measure 2-3" up from bottom of box on front and mark box at points **A**.
3. Cut across box length from **A** to **A**, and **B** to **B** as shown.
4. Cut ends of box from corner **A** to **B**.
5. Color, decorate, or cover with clear plastic shelf paper.
6. Place books inside.

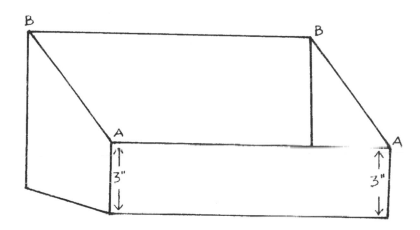

A Container for All Occasions

Classy Containers

1. Heart Basket
2. House Box
3. Cone Box
4. Treasure Chest
5. Popcorn Box
6. Box without Lid
7. Box with Lid
8. Cellophane Cone
9. Felt Bag
10. Gift Sack

This section gives you ten ideas for making all sorts of containers. For boxes, just copy pattern onto card stock, cut out, fold and glue. (You can adjust size of box by enlarging or shrinking pattern.) Decorate with markers, crayons, stickers, or stamps. Score dotted line with ruler and dull side of knife for sharp fold.

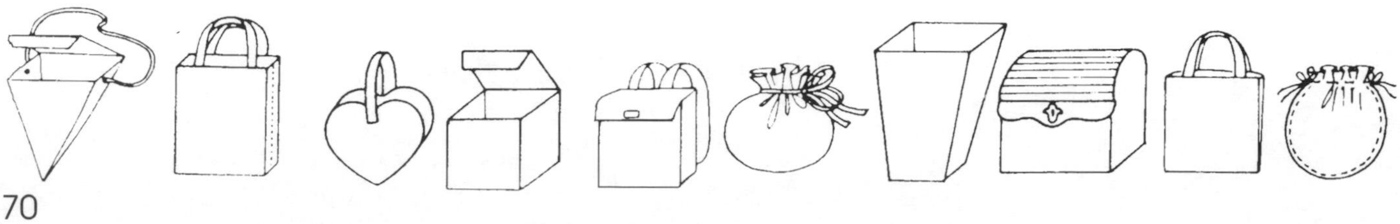

1. Heart Basket

A cute idea for Valentine's Day, Mother's Day, May Day, or just for fun.

Things You Need:

Pattern copied onto cardstock
Stapler
Pens, crayons, stickers to decorate

1. Copy pattern onto cardstock, cut out.

2. Fold in half.

3. Staple together to form a cone-shaped basket.

4. Attach handle as shown

5. Decorate with stickers, markers, or stamps.

6. Fill with a favorite treat, dried flowers, or a special gift.

2. House Box

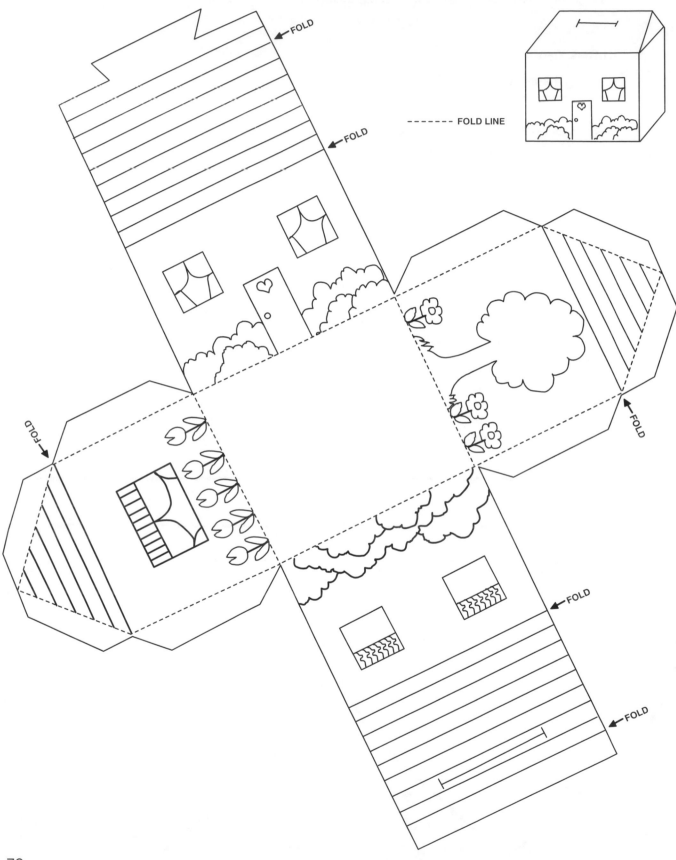

FOLD

FOLD

------ FOLD LINE

FOLD

FOLD

FOLD

FOLD

72

3. Cone Box

Add stars, hearts, and clovers to ends **A** and **C** for a new look.

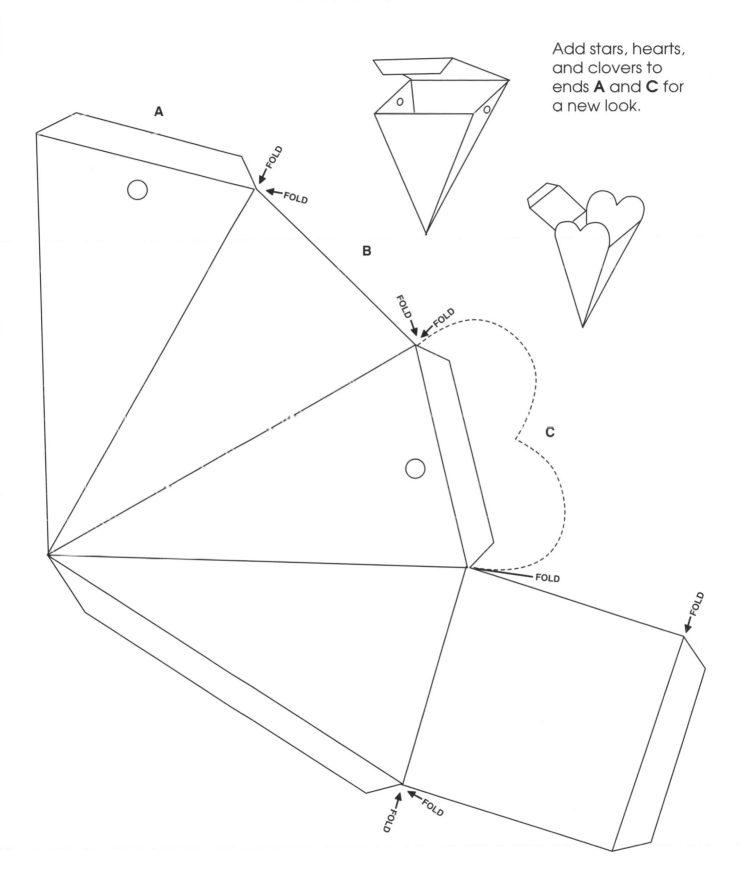

4. Treasure Chest

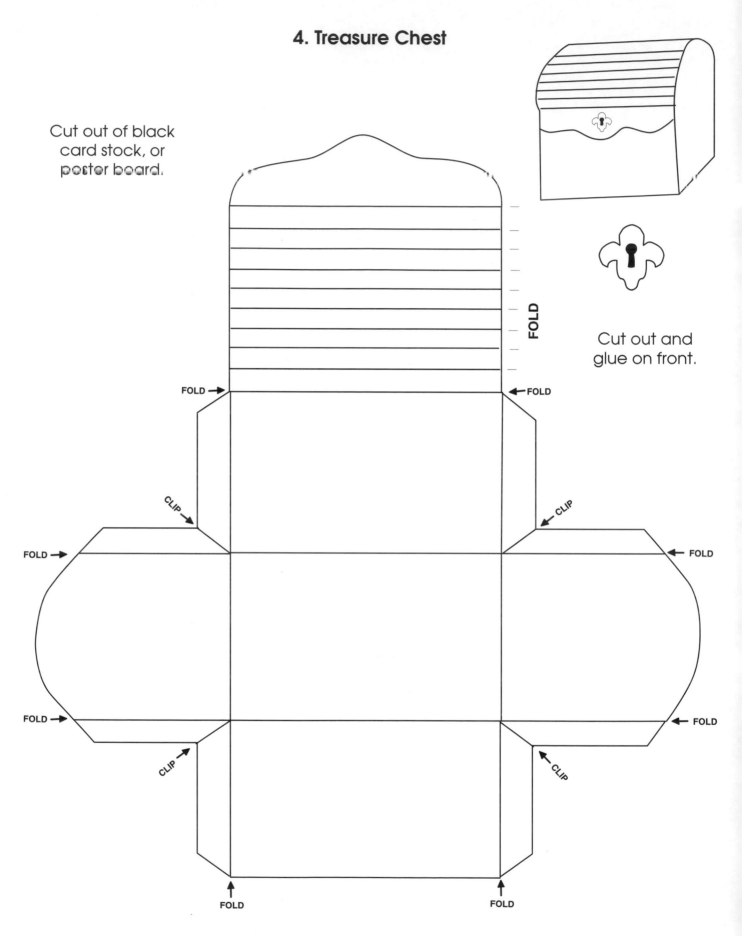

Cut out of black
card stock, or
poster board.

FOLD

Cut out and
glue on front.

FOLD

FOLD

CLIP

CLIP

FOLD

FOLD

FOLD

FOLD

CLIP

CLIP

FOLD

FOLD

CUT ———
FOLD - - - - -
SLIT ⊢——⊣

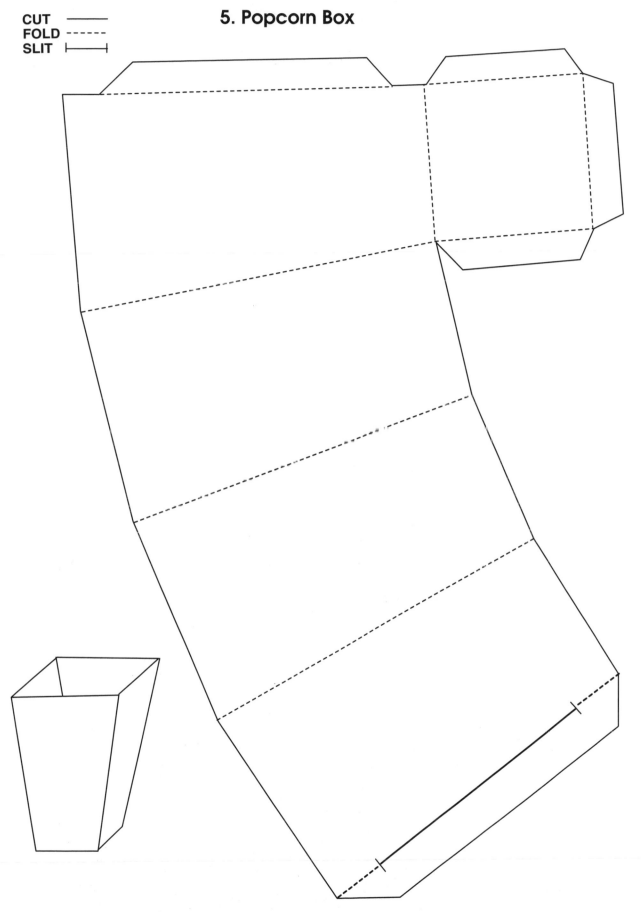

6. Box Without Lid

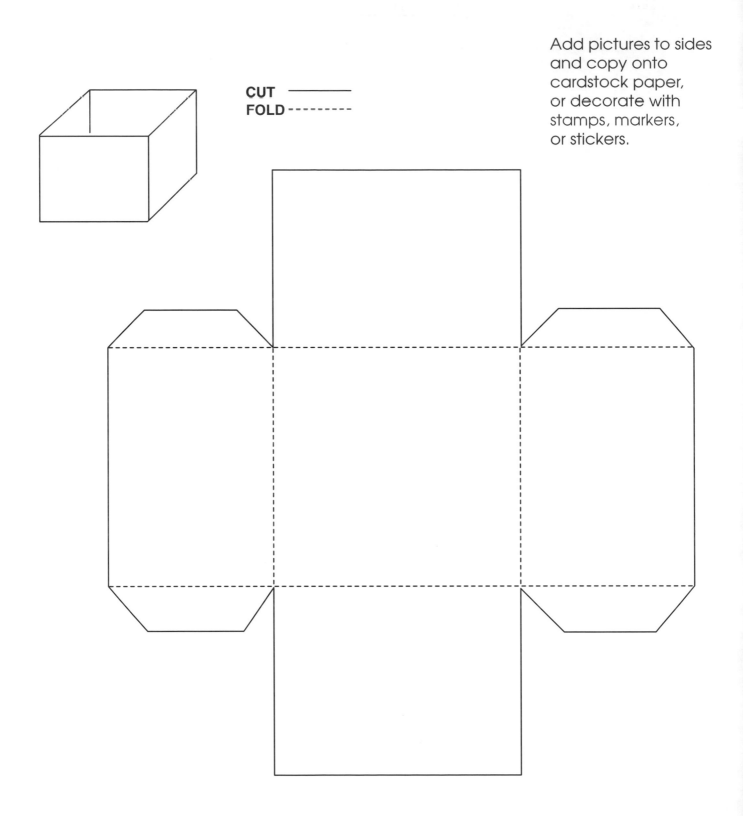

CUT ————
FOLD - - - - - - -

Add pictures to sides and copy onto cardstock paper, or decorate with stamps, markers, or stickers.

7. Box with Lid

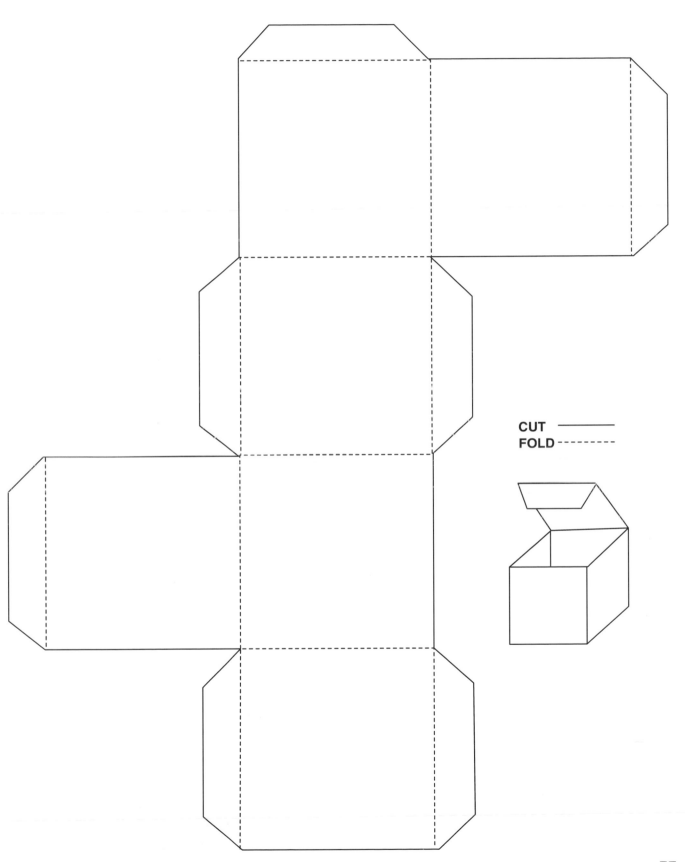

CUT ————
FOLD ----

8. Cellophane Cone

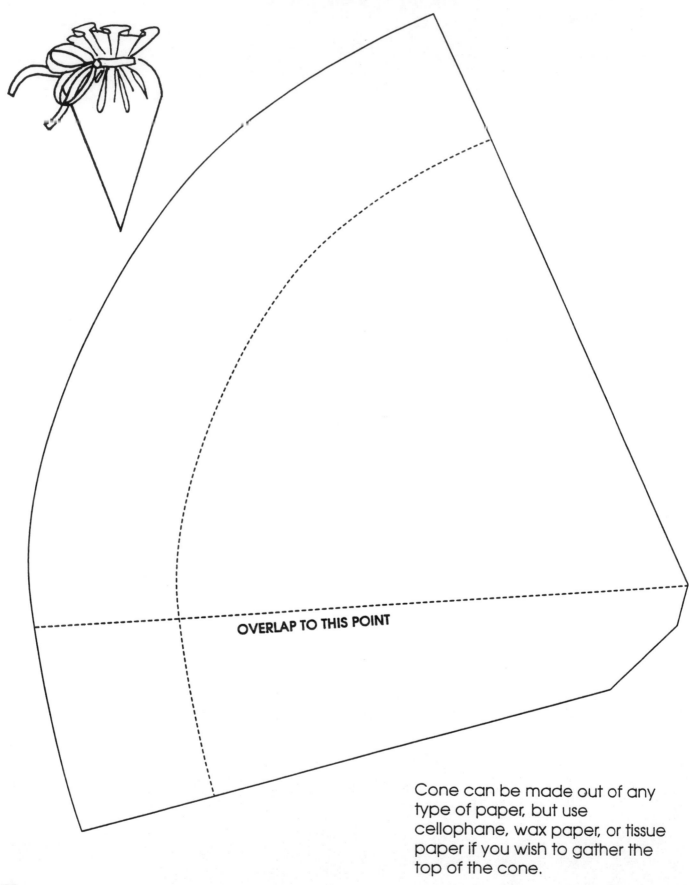

OVERLAP TO THIS POINT

Cone can be made out of any type of paper, but use cellophane, wax paper, or tissue paper if you wish to gather the top of the cone.

9. Felt Bag

- Cut pattern out of felt.
- With hole puncher, punch holes as shown.
- Thread shoelace through holes all the way around.
- Pull to gather.

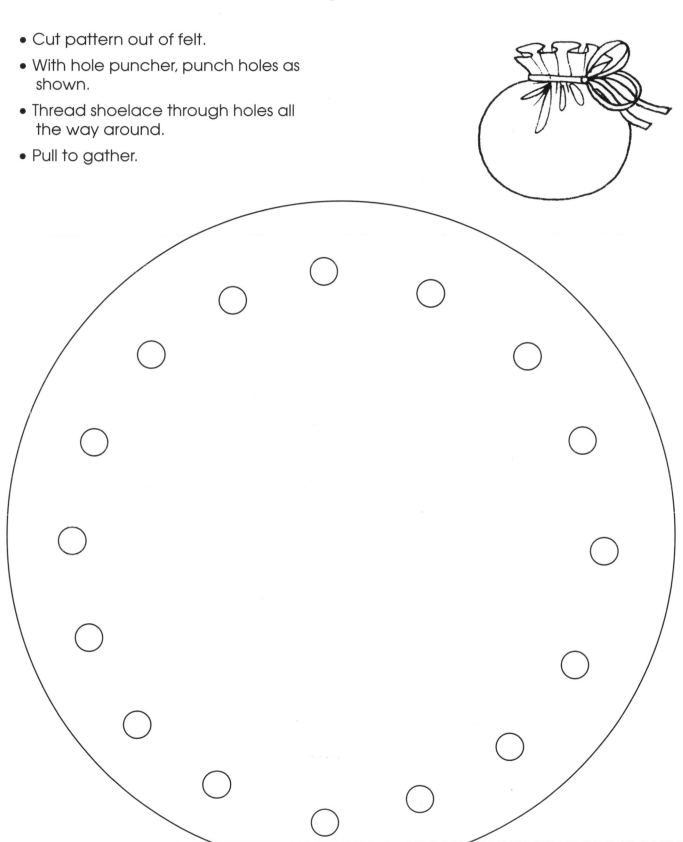

10. Gift Sack

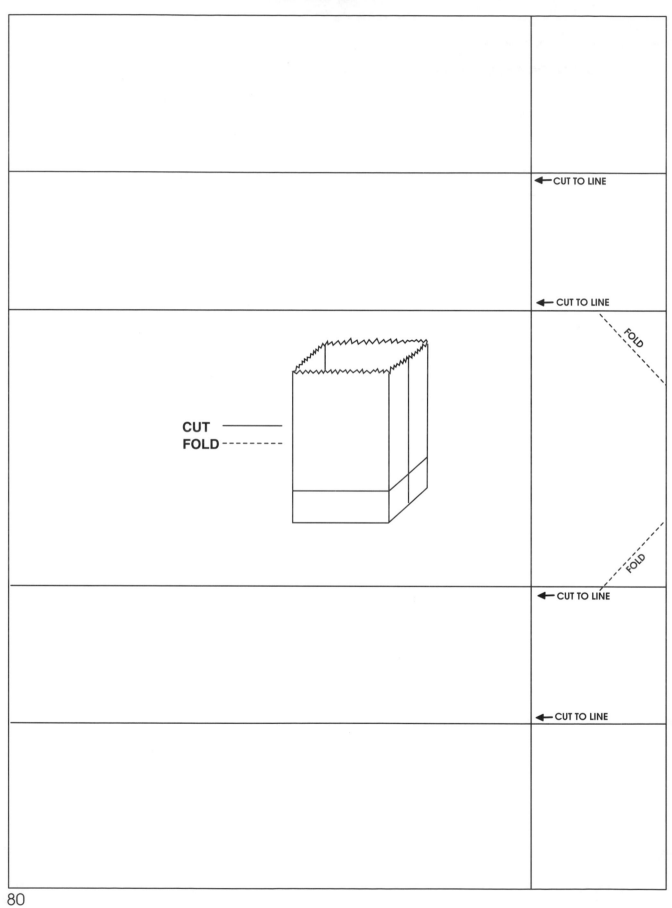

CUT ——————
FOLD - - - - - - - -

← CUT TO LINE

← CUT TO LINE

FOLD

FOLD

← CUT TO LINE

← CUT TO LINE

80

Clever Costumes

Where Imaginations Come to Life

Clever Costumes

1. Headbands — Crown, Indian, Karate, Nurse
2. Funglasses
3. Veil
4. Cape
5. Tutu
6. Bib Apron
7. Carpenter's Apron
8. ¹/2 Apron

This section gives you many ideas for fast and fun costumes. Children don't need much to let their imaginations go wild.

There are four ideas for headbands. Just copy onto cardstock and decorate, or use the basic idea to make your own.

The glasses are a very simple idea that kids absolutely love. Copy onto cardstock, cut out and color. Colored cellophane makes excellent "glass." Or, if cellophane is not available, simple plastic wrap will do. Just cut out a piece to cover the hole and glue onto the inside of the glasses.

Smocks and aprons can have many uses. Use your imagination — think of a theme and fill pockets with toys to go along with that theme. This is a great idea for an out-of-the-ordinary present.

These ideas are not just for Halloween. Use the ideas for birthday parties, school activities, home, video or play productions, or just for fun.

1. Headbands

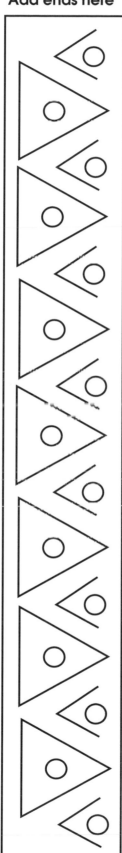

Indian
Headband

- •Add approx. 8" to each end of the Headbands using the End patterns found on the page following the Nurse and Karate Headbands.

- •Cut out of posterboard or cardstock in one piece.

- •Decorate with glitter paints, crayons, paints, or markers.

- •Put together.

Crown
Headband

83

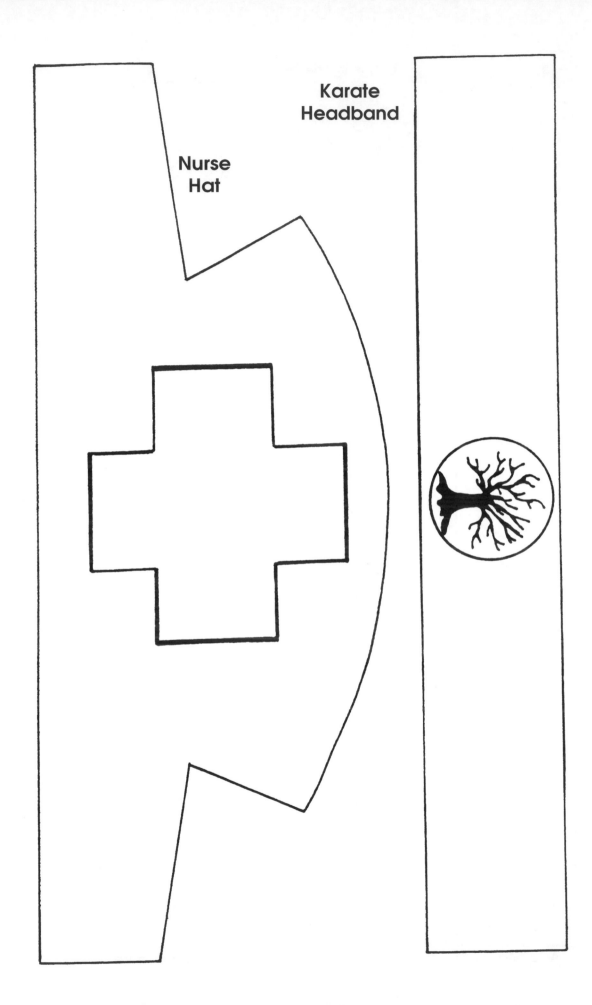

Nurse
Hat

Karate
Headband

84

End #2

End #1

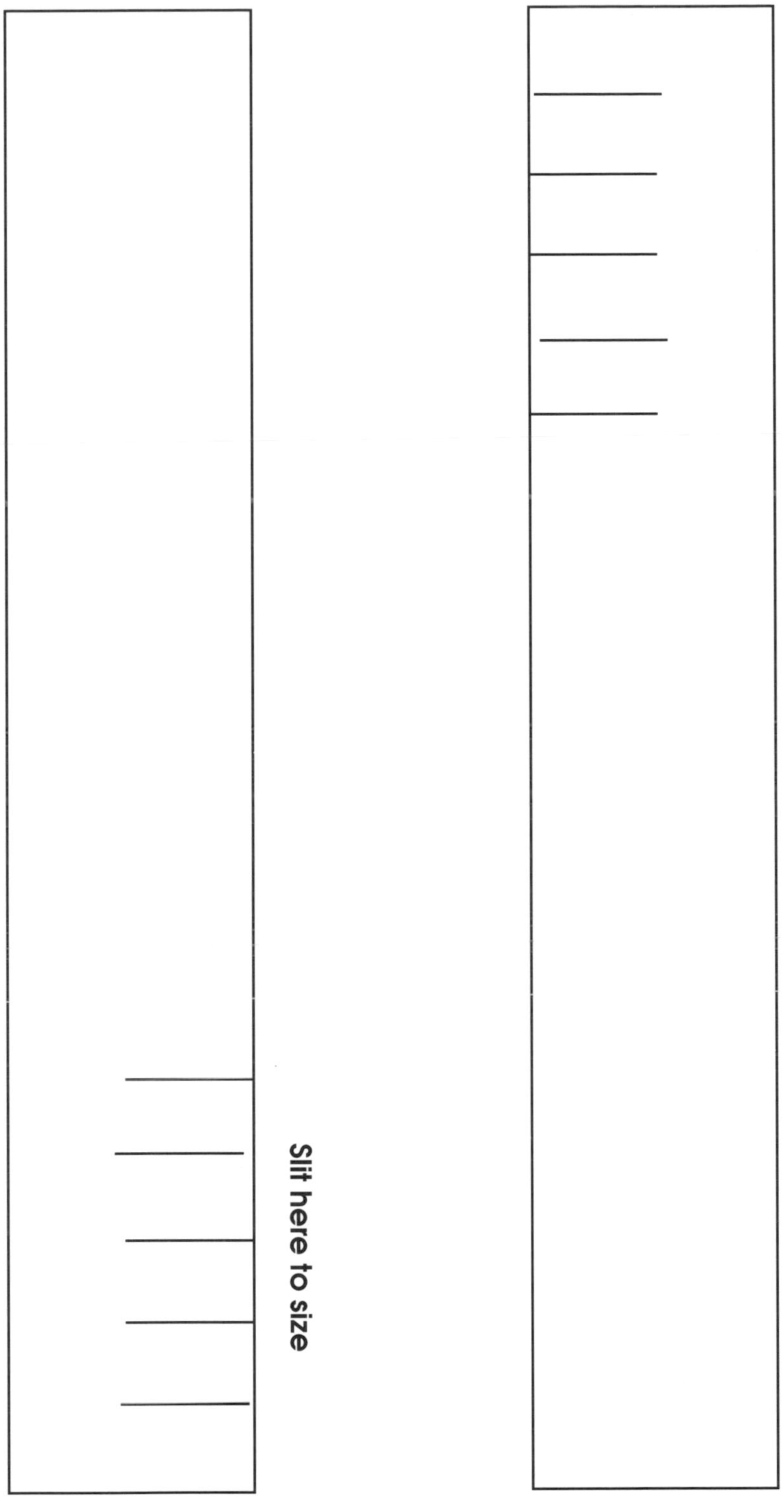

Slit here to size

Add to headband
Cut all in one piece

Add to headband
Cut all in one piece

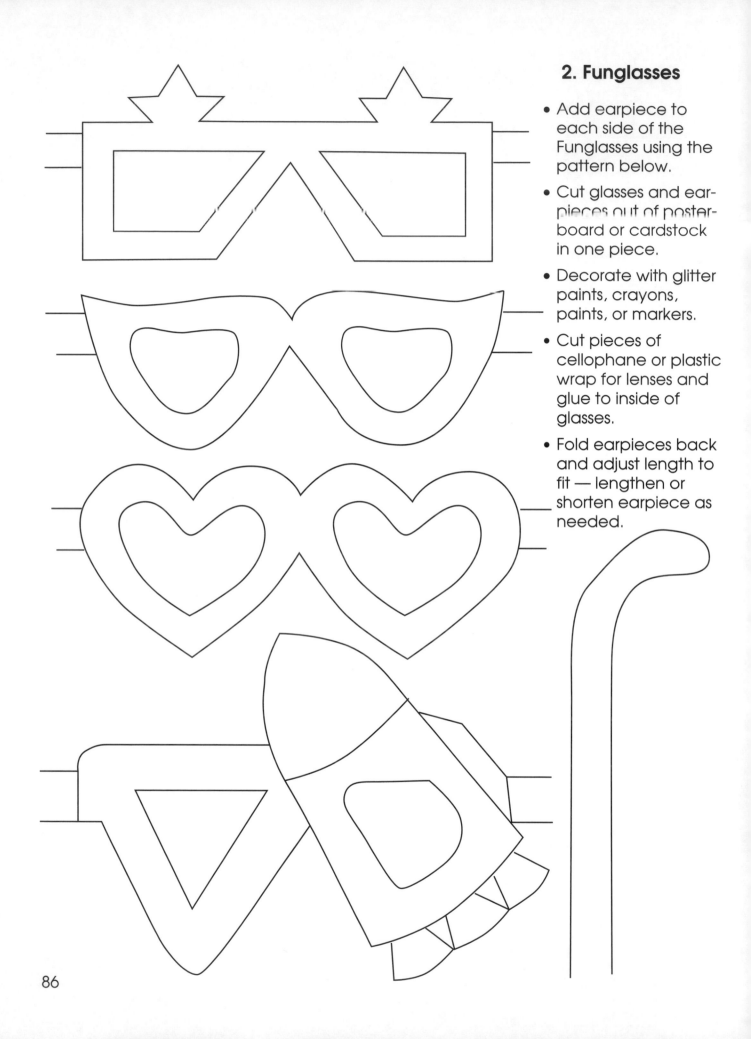

2. Funglasses

- Add earpiece to each side of the Funglasses using the pattern below.

- Cut glasses and earpieces out of posterboard or cardstock in one piece.

- Decorate with glitter paints, crayons, paints, or markers.

- Cut pieces of cellophane or plastic wrap for lenses and glue to inside of glasses.

- Fold earpieces back and adjust length to fit — lengthen or shorten earpiece as needed.

86

3. Veil

Materials Needed:

- Fabric 18" x 36" (mesh or net)
- Ribbon $1/2$" x 45"
- Flowers — plastic or silk
- Hot glue

- Gather top edge to 6".
- Sew on ribbon.
- Add flowers with hot glue.

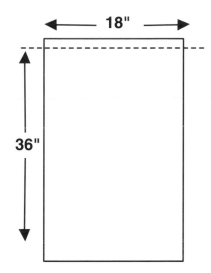

4. Cape

Materials Needed:

- Fabric 24" x 36"
- Ribbon $1/2$" x 45"

- Gather top to 12".
- Sew on ribbon.
- Hem bottom.

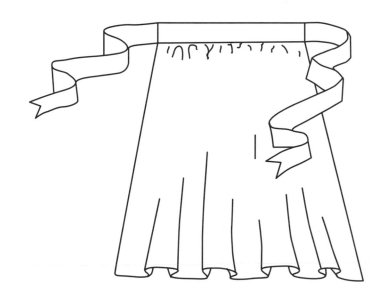

5. Tutu

Materials Needed:

- Mesh or netting 58" x 5"
- Ribbon 1" x 54"

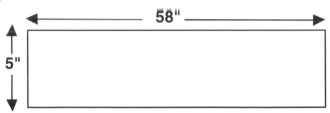

Gather top edge to 22".

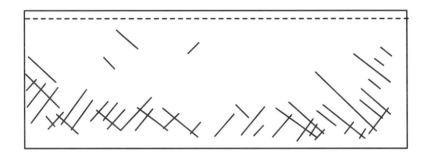

Add ribbon leaving 16" on each end.

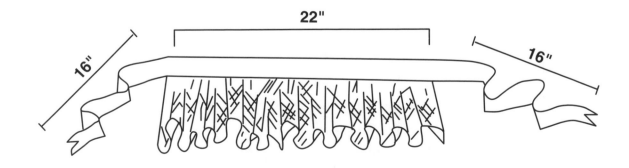

6. Bib Apron

Materials Needed:

- Fabric, canvas-type, 24" x 14"
- Ribbon 1" x 54"
- Binding (optional)

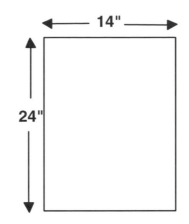

- Fold material.
- Cut out as indicated, tapering 4" to 7".

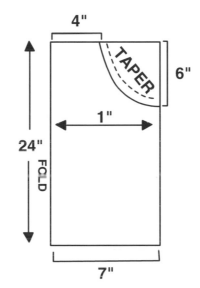

- Bind bottom edge or turn under edge.
- Fold up 5" for pockets.
- Stitch pockets.
- Bind or hem, all the way around apron.
- Add 12" ribbon to top neck edge.
- Add 14" to each side for ties.

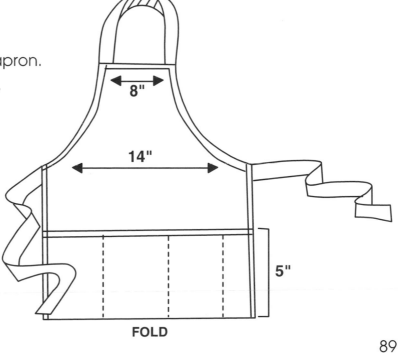

7. Carpenter's Apron

Materials Needed:

- Fabric 12" x 14" (canvas-type)
- Ribbon 1" x 18"
- Binding (optional)

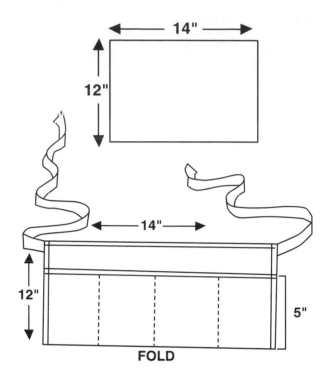

- Bind bottom edge or turn under.
- Fold up 5".
- Stitch pockets.
- Bind or turn under edges all the way around apron.
- Sew on ties.
- Use ideas for bib apron to fill pockets.

8. ½ Apron

Materials Needed:

- Fabric 36" x 18"
- Ribbon 1" x 45"

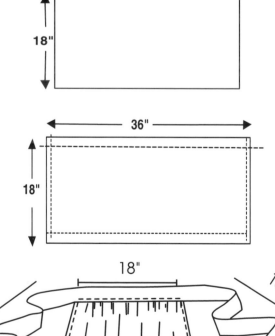

- Hem sides and bottom edges.
- Gather top edge to 18".

- Stitch ribbon along top, leaving 13½" on each side.

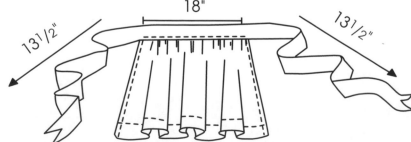

Quick Crafts

When They Can't Think of Anything to Do

When They Can't Think of Anything to Do

1. Appetizing Airplane & Tasty Train
2. Dancing Finger Puppets
3. Enchanting Eggs
4. Finger Puppets
5. Glitter Snowflakes
6. Handy Necklaces (edible)
7. Instruments for Making Music
8. Jumping Bean Bag
9. Kaleidoscope Collage
10. Little Stick Puppets
11. Magic Pudding Pictures
12. Neighborhood Map
13. Ojo de Diós (Eye of God)
14. Pinwheel
15. Sponge Stamp & Potato Press
16. Stained Glass Painting
17. Unbelievable Storybook Friends
18. Valentine Puzzle Letter
19. Windy Day Fun (WIndsock)

Creativity is an important aspect of life for everyone, but especially children. The crafts in this section are designed to be made with items you may have around the house. They are all simple and require very little time or money. These ideas were also chosen because they appeal to a wide age range. Young children need some adult help, but older children can work on their own.

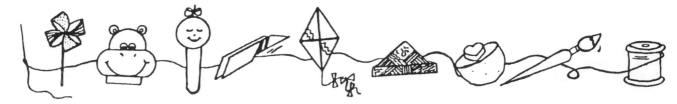

Appetizing Airplane

Things You Need:

- 1 elastic
- 1 stick of gum
- 2 LifeSavers®
- 1 roll of Smarties® or Tootsie Roll®

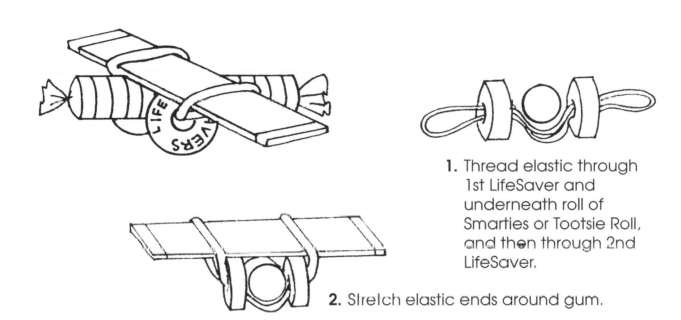

1. Thread elastic through 1st LifeSaver and underneath roll of Smarties or Tootsie Roll, and then through 2nd LifeSaver.

2. Stretch elastic ends around gum.

Tasty Train

Things You Need:

- 1 package of LifeSavers (middle)
- 1 package of gum (bottom)
- 4 wrapped round mints (wheels)
- 1 chocolate Kiss® (smoke stack)
- 1 square package candy
- Hot-glue and/or tape

1. Hot-glue mints on pack of gum.

2. Glue LifeSavers on gum and candy and kiss on top of LifeSavers.

Dancing Finger Puppets

Things You Need:

- Paper
- Scissors
- Crayons

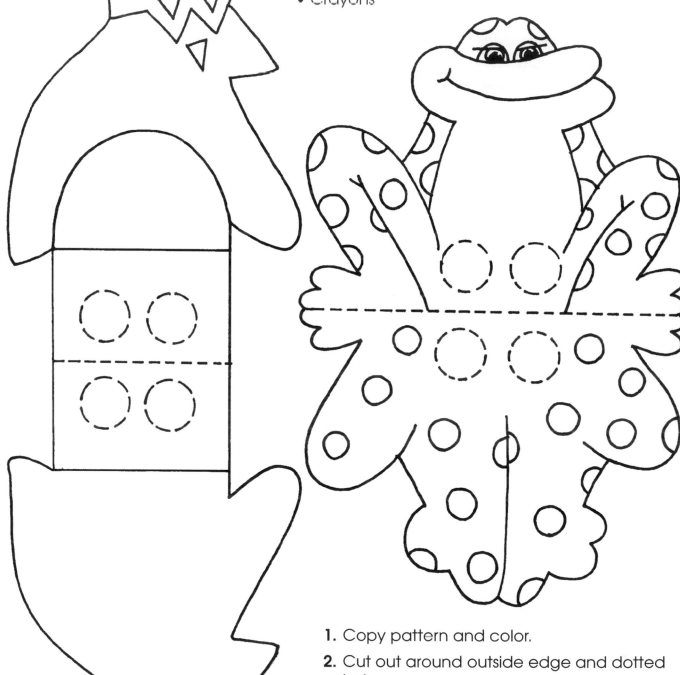

1. Copy pattern and color.
2. Cut out around outside edge and dotted holes.
3. Fold along dotted line in center.
4. Insert fingers through holes for legs, then make the puppet dance with fingers.

94

Enchanting Eggs

Things You Need:

- Eggs
- Markers

1. Hard boil eggs.

2. Allow eggs to cool completely.

3. Decorate eggs with markers, paint and/or stickers. Refrigerate the same as regular hard boiled eggs.

Finger Puppets

Things You Need:

- Assorted Felt
- Scissors
- Glue
- Pompoms and plastic eyes

1. Cut out of different colors of felt.

2. Glue back to front just on edges.

3. Use pompoms for features marked (P) and plastic eyes (available at craft stores).

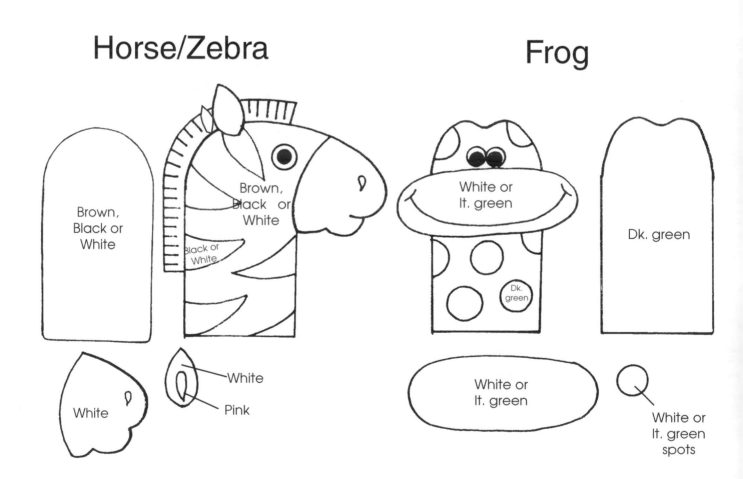

Horse/Zebra

Brown, Black or White

Brown, Black or White

Black or White

White

White

Pink

Frog

White or lt. green

Dk. green

Dk. green

White or lt. green

White or lt. green spots

Owl

Finger Puppets

Hippo

Brown

Brown

Pink

Gray

Pink

Gray

White

Orange

Mouse

White

White

Fox/Dog

P

Pink

Pink

White

Gray

Gray

P

White

Brown or red

Brown   or red

Cat

White

Bear

Orange

P   P

Orange

Black

P

White

Brown

Brown

Glitter Snowflakes

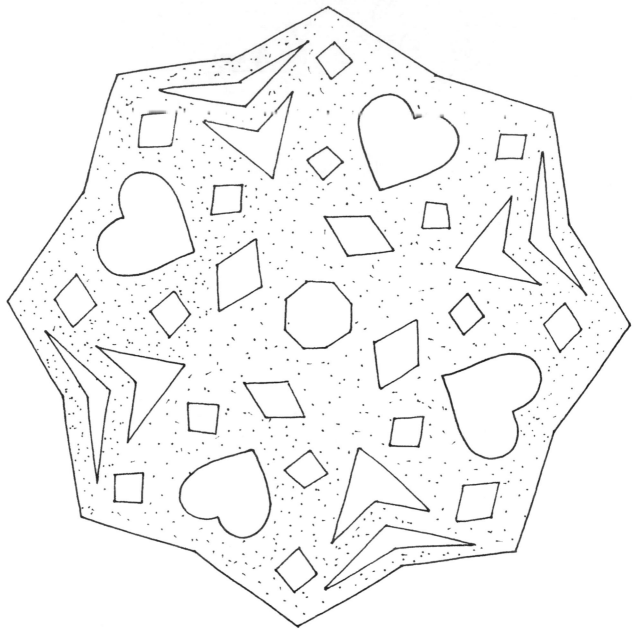

Things You Need:

- 1 stick paraffin wax
- Tissue Paper
- Glitter

1. Melt wax in pan on low heat.

2. Add glitter.

3. Make snowflakes out of tissue paper.

4. Set snowflakes in wax and glitter. Remove when covered and let dry on wax paper. Hang in window for a beautiful decoration.

Handy Necklaces
(edible)

Things You Need:

- Yarn, ribbon, or thread and needle, scotch tape
- Marshmallows, raisins, fruit or oat ring cereal, noodles, or jelly beans.

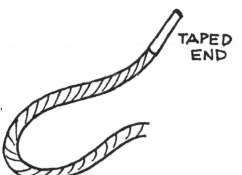

TAPED END

1. If using ribbon or yarn, tape one end for needle.

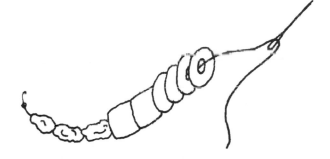

2. Thread on cereal, noodles, or sew on raisins or marshmallows.

3. Tie ends — fun for all occasions.

Instruments for Making Music

Be-Boppin' Bells

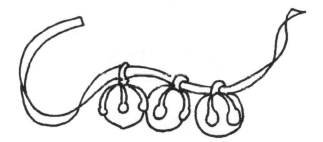

- Bells
- Ribbon or shoelace

Tie on shoes, ankles, or wrists.

Musical Maracas

- Paper cup
- Heavy Paper
- Popcorn
- Tape

Fill cup with small amount of popcorn.
Cut circle out of heavy paper to fit top of cup.
Tape all across top.
Shake.

Tango Tambourine

- 2 plates
- Popcorn
- Tape

Fill plate with small amount of popcorn.
Tape second plate over top.
Shake and hit.

Twinkling Triangle

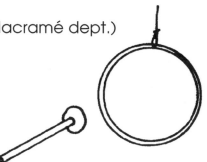

- Metal ring (purchase at a craft store in Macramé dept.)
- String
- Dowel $1/4$" x 8"
- 1" bead with $1/4$" hole

Tie string to ring to hold by.
Glue bead to dowel for mallet.

Instruments for Making Music (cont'd.)

Thumping Drum

- Oatmeal box

Decorate, if desired. Beat on top.

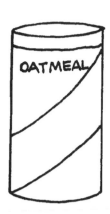

Super Sandpaper Blocks

- 2 – 2" x 4" x 4" blocks of wood
- Sandpaper (fine or medium)

Glue sandpaper on blocks.
Hit blocks together as you move them back and forth.

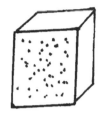
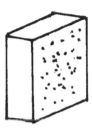

Silly Sticks

- Cut 2 – 8" x 1/2" dowels

Rubber Band Racket

- Shoebox lid
- Rubber bands

Stretch elastics either way around lid.
Strum like a guitar.

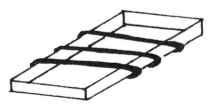

Pop Stompers

- Pop cans
- Stomp on feet and walk (best used outside)

Jumping Bean Bag

Things You Need:

- Old socks
- Yarn
- Dry beans and corn kernels

1. Fill bottom of sock with beans.

2. Tie sock shut with yarn.

  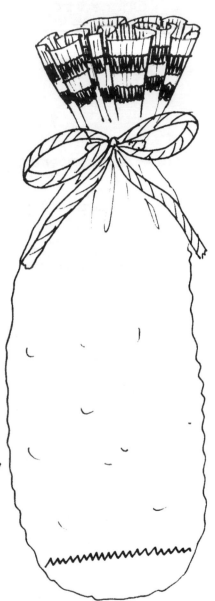

Kaleidoscope Collage

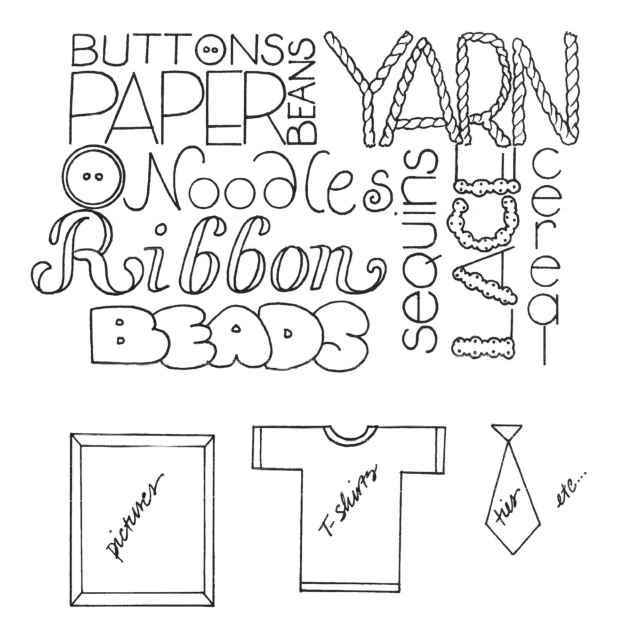

Things You Need:

- Paper, cardboard, or board
- Glue
- Noodles, paper, buttons, beads, yarn, sequins
- Cereal, dry beans, rice

1. Cover paper with glue.

2. Make a beautiful creation by covering glue with all sorts of things.

3. Let dry.

Collage T-Shirts

This also works on T-shirts or ties. Use fabric paint in squirt bottles to glue on beads, material, buttons, lace, or ribbon. Let dry 24 hours. Hand wash and drip dry.

Little Stick Puppets

Things You Need:

- Paper
- Ice Pop Sticks
- Glue
- Scissors

1. Copy.
2. Color.
3. Cut out.
4. Glue on ice pop sticks or tongue depressors.

104

Magic Pudding Pictures

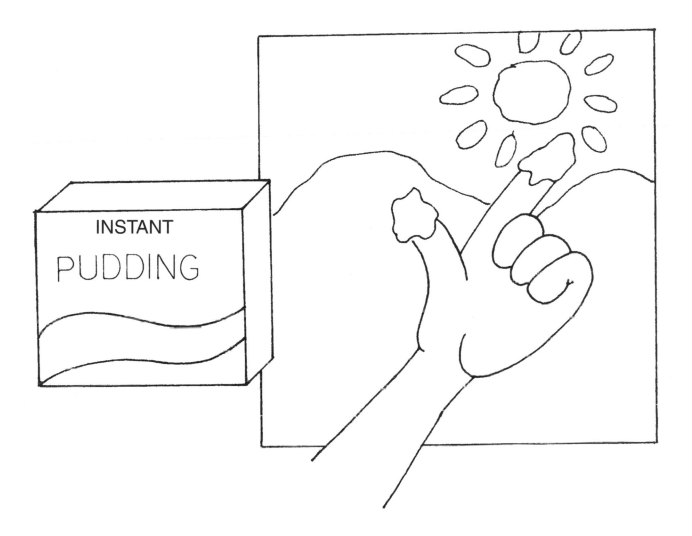

Things You Need:

- 1 package instant pudding
- 2 large pieces of paper

1. Mix pudding according to package directions.

2. Use fingers to create a 3-dimensional picture with pudding as paint.

3. Let dry.

Neighborhood Map

Things You Need:
- Paper
- Crayons

1. Draw out a map of neighborhood including parks, stores, gas stations, and ponds.

2. Color and laminate map.

3. Let children use small cars to drive on map. (Make a few of these and insert in a book or folder to take on vacation).

Ojo de Diós (Eye of God)

Materials Needed:

- 2 sticks 8" long, or 2 plastic straws
- Colored yarn

1. Tie sticks together to form a cross using a very long piece of yarn.

2. Using same piece of yarn, loop around arm 1 and head 2, then arm 3, then 4. Keep yarn tight as you loop around sticks and push toward center.

3. When yarn runs out, tie it to another piece of yarn and keep going. Use different colors for extra luck.

4. When sticks are full, tie the yarn to one of the sticks.

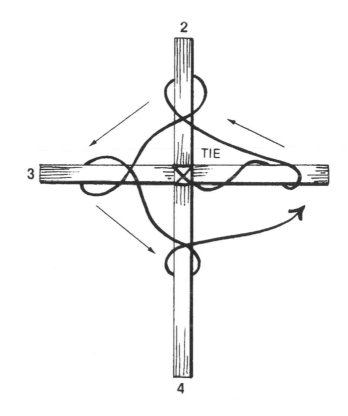

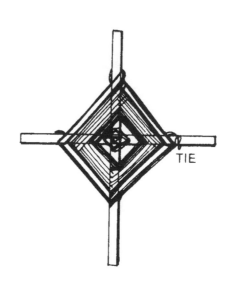

Pinwheel

A great Spring project or a fun birthday favor.

Things You Need:

- Colored paper with pattern
- 1 pin
- 1 straw
- An eraser or small cork

1. Copy pattern onto colored paper. Cut out square. Cut along dotted lines to center circle, making sure not to cut through circle.

2. Take each corner marked **X** and bend it into the circle. Hold with finger.

3. Push the pin through each corner and through center circle. Then push the pin through a straw, then an eraser or piece of cork.

pin

BACK OF PINWHEEL

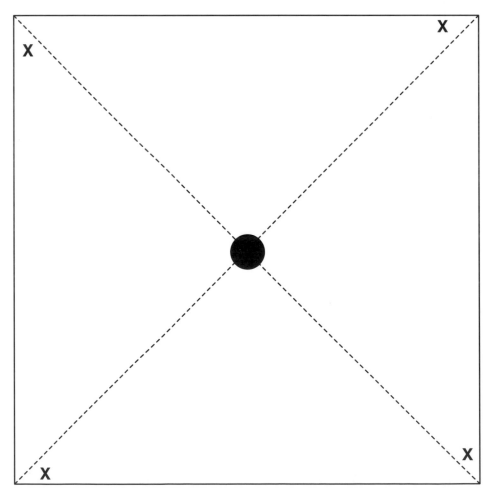

Sponge Stamp and Potato Press

Things You Need:

- Potato or sponge
- Paint
- Knife or scissors

Sponge Stamp

1. Cut sponge in desired shapes using scissors.

2. Dip sponge shapes in acrylic paints and decorate cards, wrapping paper, clothes, and shoes.

3. Compressed sponges in various shapes are available at craft stores.

Potato Press

1. Cut potato in half.

2. Draw design on sponge.

3. Cut out with knife — adult supervision required.

4. Dip design in acrylic paint and decorate cards, wrapping paper, or T-shirts, by pressing potato onto item.

Basic Shape Ideas

Stained Glass Painting

Things You Need:

- ¹/₂ cup corn syrup
- Food coloring

1. Mix food coloring into corn syrup until desired color is obtained.

2. Paint picture on paper.

3. Let dry several days before hanging.

Unbelievable Storybook Friends

Rowdy Rabbit

Things You Need:

- Pompoms
- Glue
- Assortment of felt and ribbon
- Wiggly eyes
- Felt for ears and teeth

Crazy Cat

Wiggly eyes

o   Black beads — for dragon

○ $1/8$" pompom

○ $1/4$" pompom

○ $1/2$" pompom

Pretty Pig

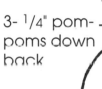

Bouncy Bear

3- $1/4$" pom-
poms down
back

1" to $1^1/2$"
pompom for
head

Mysterious Mouse

Dingy Dragon

Dutiful Dog

1. As shown in the pictures, glue
   pompoms together.

2. Glue felt and eyes onto pompoms.

- You can use these fun animals to
  make hand puppets by gluing one
  animal onto each finger of a glove.

- These can become stick puppets by
  gluing onto ice pop sticks.

- Try gluing onto the end of a cute
  pencil for an extra special surprise.

Dancing Deer

Valentine Puzzle Letter

**Valentine's Day,
Father's Day, or
Mother's Day**

Birthday

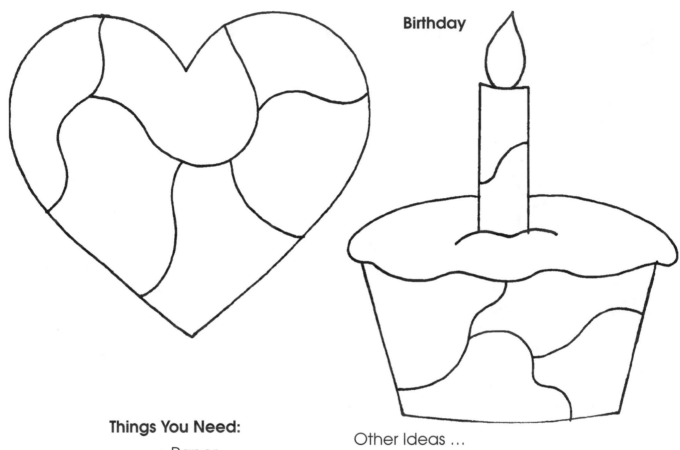

Things You Need:

- Paper
- Pens

Other Ideas …

Christmas Tree or Star
Pumpkin or Ghost
Moon, Fish, or Kite

1. Outline your desired shape on paper.

2. Write letter keeping all writing within shape.

3. Cut out shape and cut letter into puzzle shapes.

4. Mail letter — when it is received, it will have to be put together so it can be read.

Windy Day Fun
(Windsock)

Things You Need:

- 1 piece of 8$\frac{1}{2}$" x 11" cardstock
- Pens, stickers, and paints to decorate
- Crepe paper cut in strips
- Yarn or string
- Scissors, glue, tape
- Stapler

1. Decorate cardstock as desired.

   Roll and glue to form a tube.

2. Punch 2 holes at top across from each other.

   Tie piece of yarn or ribbon to hang.

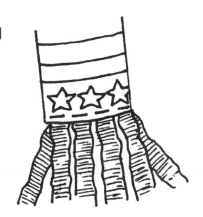

3. Take strips of 12" long crepe paper and staple to bottom all the way around.

   Hang outside or inside.

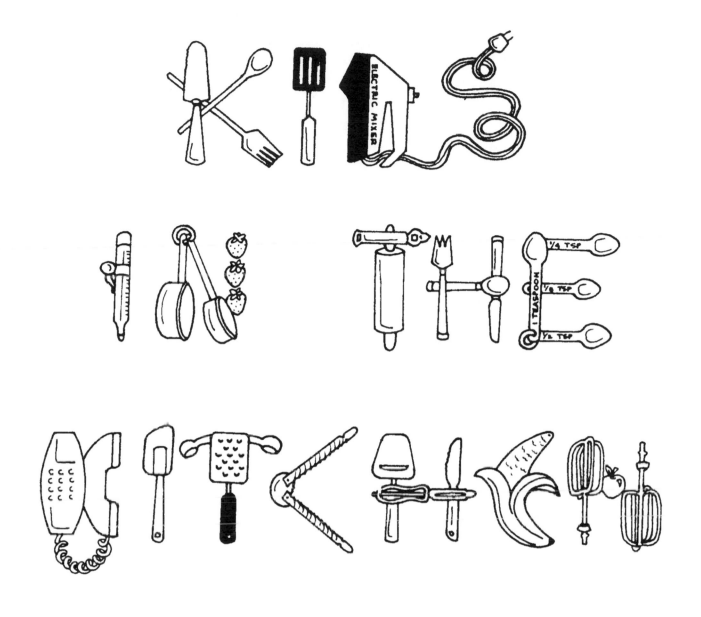

KIDS IN THE KITCHEN

Recipes Especially for Children

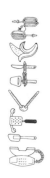

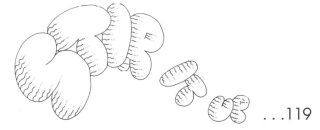
KIDS IN THE KITCHEN

Table of Contents

1. Peanut Butter Funny Faces
2. Frozen Cupcakes
3. Cream Cheese Candies
4. The Easiest Fudge in the World
5. Yummy Peanut Butter Balls
6. Flavored Popcorn
7. Honey Yum Yums
8. Nutty Dough
9. English Muffin Pizzas
10. Fun Ice Cubes
11. Trail Mix
12. Yummy Yogurt Ice Pops
13. Fancy Frutti Ice Sparkle
14. Orange Ice Cream Pops
15. Frozen Bananas
16. Bugs On A Log
17. Fruit Shish Kabobs
18. Healthy Apple Leather
19. Frozen Fruit Salad
20. Chocolate Pie
21. Chocolate Covered Peanut Butter Balls
22. Easy No-Bake Chocolate Cake
23. Sweet Cereal Mix
24. Personal Cheese Pizzas
25. Applesauce Whip
26. Snow Cones
27. My Favorite Recipe

1. Dish Soap Bubbles
2. Kitchen Clay
3. Play Dough
4. Oblique
5. Salt Beads
6. Papier Mâché Flour Paste
7. Sticker Stuff
8. Salt Dough
9. Liquid Starch Fingerpaint
10. Moldable Soap
11. Corn Starch Modeling Clay
12. Stain Glass Paint

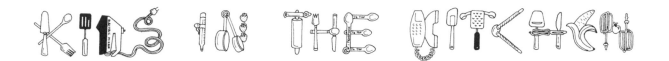

Introduction

There is magic in creating something wonderful to eat and then enjoying it with your children. In today's busy world, we often don't have time to go through the elaborate process of cooking with our children, but we need not deprive them of this enjoyable experience.

The first section of this chapter, **Stir It Up**, is devoted to giving parents and children many *very* easy recipes that require little time, preparation, or mess. With minimal effort, children can create delicious dishes and enjoy the rewards of cooking.

Also included in this chapter is the section entitled, **Shake, Rattle & Roll**, which contains twelve essential and fun craft recipes children need. These ideas are useful for school assignments, art projects, or just exploring one's creativity on a rainy Saturday afternoon.

Pages can be copied onto cardstock and cut to fit into your recipe card holders, or given with a treat as a gift. Laminate for long lasting cards.

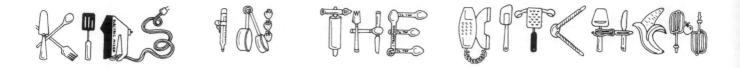

KIDS IN THE KITCHEN

The kids said, "Let's make cookies."
"No problem," was my reply
I can handle this I thought
On my patience I must rely.

We need 3 cups of flour,
One cup ended on the floor.
"Mom, I want to measure the salt."
"Hey, it's not his turn to pour!"

"I'll get the eggs," said one little voice,
as they cracked all over the table.
I won't get angry, I said to myself,
I really am much too stable.

The butter didn't make it to the bowl,
It got all over the chair.
When sister started to mix the dough,
The beaters got caught in her hair.

One teaspoon full of soda does not mean soda pop.
"Who spilled the dough onto the floor?"
"Would someone please get me a mop?"

"She had one more taste than me!"
"Did not!" — "Did so!" — "Did not!"
I won't get mad, I won't, I won't,
But I think my nerves are shot.

I'm not sure how good they'll taste
When the cookies are all done.
The kitchen's a mess, my patience is gone
But the kids are having fun.

Delicious and Easy Recipes
Especially for Children to Make

Children love to make things without help from an adult. The following recipes were collected especially for children. There is no cooking, no need for sharp knives, boiling water, or mixers. They are all very simply done with wonderful results. Parents should always supervise, but these recipes will need minimal "hands-on" help.

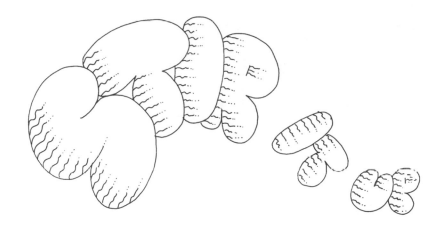

1. Peanut Butter Funny Faces
2. Frozen Cupcakes
3. Cream Cheese Candies
4. The Easiest Fudge in the World
5. Yummy Peanut Butter Balls
6. Flavored Popcorn
7. Honey Yum Yums
8. Nutty Dough
9. English Muffin Pizzas
10. Fun Ice Cubes
11. Trail Mix
12. Yummy Yogurt Ice Pops
13. Fancy Frutti Ice Sparkle
14. Orange Ice Cream Pops
15. Frozen Bananas
16. Bugs On A Log
17. Fruit Shish Kabobs
18. Healthy Apple Leather
19. Frozen Fruit Salad
20. Chocolate Pie
21. Chocolate Covered Peanut Butter Balls
22. Easy No-Bake Chocolate Cake
23. Sweet Cereal Mix
24. Personal Cheese Pizzas
25. Applesauce Whip
26. Snow Cones
27. My Favorite Recipe

1.

Peanut Butter Funny Faces — They will Make You Laugh
(5 minutes)

You will need: bread
                  peanut butter
                  raisins, little marshmallows, chocolate chips
                  jam

1. Spread peanut butter onto bread.
2. Spread jam in a circle on top of peanut butter.
3. Use raisins, to make eyes, nose, and mouth.

2.

Frozen Cupcakes — Frosty and Delicious
(15 minutes plus freezing time)

You will need: 1 cup plain yogurt
                  1/8 cup honey
                  1 16 oz. can whole cranberry sauce
                  1 8 oz. can crushed pineapple

1. Line 2 muffin tins with cupcake papers.
2. Mix yogurt and honey in a bowl.
3. Add cranberry sauce and pineapple — Stir.
4. Pour mixture into muffin cups.

Put muffin pan In freezer until frozen.
Thaw five minutes before eating.

3.

Cream Cheese Candies — You Won't Believe It's This Easy
(10 minutes)

You will need: 1 3 oz. pkg. cream cheese, softened
                  3 cups powdered sugar
                  food coloring (optional)
                  1/2 tsp. peppermint extract (optional)

1. Combine cream cheese and extract in bowl.
2. Gradually beat in powdered sugar until smooth (knead in any remaining sugar if necessary to have a firm dough).
3. Add food coloring if desired.
4. Roll pieces into small balls and flatten or roll in granulated sugar and press into molds.

Place onto wax paper and let dry. Makes 6-8 dozen.

4.

The Easiest Fudge in the World — Delicious, Too!
(10 minutes)

You will need: 1 14 oz. can sweetened condensed milk
 1 12 oz. pkg. chocolate chips
 1 tsp. vanilla
 1/2 cup chopped nuts, if desired

1. Butter a 9" square baking pan.
2. In microwave bowl, combine milk and chocolate chips. Microwave on medium about 2 min. (until chocolate is soft).
3. Remove from microwave and stir until smooth.
4. Stir in vanilla and nuts.
5. Pour into pan.

Refrigerate 2 hours or until firm. Cut into pieces.

5.

Yummy Peanut Butter Balls — Fun to Make and Good to Eat!
(15 minutes)

You will need: 1 cup peanut butter
 1/2 cup wheat germ
 1 cup raisins
 1/2 cup coconut

1. Mix first 3 ingredients together.
2. Form into balls.
3. Roll in coconut.

Refrigerate.

6.

Flavored Popcorn — Colorful and Yummy!
(10 minutes)

You will need: 8 cups popped corn
 1/2 c. melted butter
 1 pkg. gelatin

1. Place popcorn in a clean sack.
2. Pour butter over popcorn. Close sack and shake.
3. Sprinkle gelatin over popcorn. Close sack and shake gently.

7.

Honey Yum Yums — A Delicious and Healthy Snack
(15 minutes)

You will need: 1 c. peanut butter
1 c. honey
2 c. powdered milk
$1/2$ c. coconut

1. Mix together.
2. Roll into balls.
3. Place on wax paper until set.

8.

Nutty Dough — Fun to Play With and Good to Eat
(15 minutes)

You will need: 3 cups peanut butter
4 cups powdered sugar
3 $1/2$ cups honey
4 cups powdered milk

1. Mix ingredients together.
2. Roll into balls or wash your hands and play with dough. You can make all sorts of things. Use raisins, cereal, or anything else you can think of to decorate your creations. Then eat them all up.

9.

English Muffin Pizzas — Make Fun Personal Pizzas!
(5 minutes)

You will need: English muffins
tomato sauce
cheese

1. Spoon tomato sauce onto English muffins.
2. Cover with grated cheese.
3. Place in microwave for 30 seconds.

10.

Fun Ice Cubes

For a fun surprise drink, make ice-cubes with something special inside. Fill ice-cube tray with water and put a surprise in each cube, then freeze.

On Halloween, try little plastic spiders or green grapes for vampire eyes.

For Valentine's Day slice strawberries lengthwise to look like hearts.

11.

Trail Mix — Much Better Than Candy!
(10 min.)

You will need: 2 c. small chocolate candies
2 c. raisins
2 c. peanuts
2 c. pretzels
2 c. shelled raw sunflower seeds

1. Mix together in bowl.
2. Other things to add if you want: coconut, dried fruit, peanut butter chips, bite-sized cereal.

12.

Yummy Yogurt Ice Pops — Refreshing and Good For You

You will need: 1 quart yogurt
1 large can frozen orange juice concentrate
1/4 cup honey

1. Mix together.
2. Freeze in ice pop molds or paper cups with sticks.

13.

Fancy Frutti Ice Sparkle — A Frosty Way to Quench Your Thirst
(10 minutes)

You will need: 3 1 oz. pkgs. of powdered drink mix
(any flavor or combination of flavors)
Chilled lemon-lime soda

1. According to directions, mix each package separately and pour into ice cube trays.
2. When frozen, put 2 or 3 cubes of each flavor in glass and pour soda over.

14.

Orange Ice Cream Pops — Cool and Creamy
(15 minutes + freezing time)

You will need: ice pop sticks
1 cup milk
1 6 oz. can frozen orange juice concentrate
(partly thawed)
1 pint vanilla ice cream

1. Mix all ingredients together in blender or with a wire whisk, blend until smooth.
2. Pour into 3 ¹/₂ oz. paper cups.
3. Place in freezer until firm (insert ice pop sticks into cup when partially frozen).

15.

Frozen Bananas — A Great Snack for Anytime!
(20 minutes)

You will need: bananas
ice pop sticks
1 c. lemon juice or orange juice
1 c. chocolate chips
chopped peanuts or walnuts and coconut

1. Cut bananas in half and insert ice pop sticks.
2. Roll banana in juice, put on wax paper.
3. Set in freezer until firm.
4. Melt chocolate chips in microwave until soft (1–2 min.)
5. Spoon chocolate over bananas and roll in nuts or coconut (or both).
Other variations: Spread with honey, peanut butter, or marshmallow creme, roll in wheat germ, grape-nuts or other cereal.

16.

Bugs On a Log

You will need: celery
         peanut butter   raisins
         cream cheese   chocolate chips
         cheese spread   olives

1. Fill celery with peanut butter, cream cheese, or cheese spread.
2. Place raisins, olives, or chocolate chips on top for bugs.

17.

Fruit Shish Kabobs
(15 minutes)

These shish kabobs require no cutting — a perfect, healthy treat for even the youngest kids to make all by themselves.

You will need: grapes — green and red
         Mandarin oranges
         Maraschino cherries
         strawberries

Alternate fruit onto spears. Experiment with colors and patterns. A great way to teach kids their colors and how to make patterns.

18.

Healthy Apple Leather

You will need: 1 jar applesauce

1. Cover cookie sheet with heat-resistant plastic wrap. Tape to edges with masking tape.
2. Pour applesauce 1/4 inch thick. Spread evenly.
3. Put in oven at 140° F with oven door slightly open. Dry applesauce several hours until it is leathery. Some people like it dried longer until it is crispy. Either way it is delicious and nutritious. Better than candy.

Other puréed fruit is great, too.

19.

 Frozen Fruit Salad
(20 minutes)

You will need: 1 small pkg. gelatin — your favorite flavor
1 12 oz. whipped topping, thawed
1 6 oz. frozen orange juice concentrate
1 can drained crushed pineapple
1 10 1/2 oz. can canned fruit — your favorite

1. Mix together gelatin and whipped topping until smooth.
2. Add fruit and juice — mix.
3. Put into the refrigerator until it is set.

20.

Chocolate Pie — A Quick and Delicious Pie Even a Child Can Make!
(15 minutes + freezing time)

You will need: 1 cup chocolate chips
1 12 oz. whipped topping, thawed
1 9" chocolate cookie pie crust

1. Melt chocolate chips in microwave until soft (1–2 min.).
2. Stir until smooth, then mix in whipped topping — carefully mix together and pour into pie crust.
3. Chill until set.

21.

Chocolate Covered Peanut Butter Balls — Absolutely Wonderful!

You will need: 1 cup butter
2 cups peanut butter
3 cups powdered sugar
2 1/2 cups chocolate chips

1. Melt butter in microwave.
2. Mix peanut butter and powdered sugar into butter.
3. Roll into small balls and place on wax paper.
4. Melt chocolate in microwave.
5. Drop balls into chocolate and place on wax paper. Let dry.

22.

Easy No-Bake Chocolate Cake
— They'll Think You Spent Hours on This One! —

You will need: 1 8 oz. container frozen whipped topping, thawed
or 2 cups whipped cream
1 pkg. chocolate cookies

1. Spread whipped topping on each wafer and stack on top of each other (make 4 or 5 stacks).
2. Lay stacks down on side and put all stacks together to form one long roll.
3. Frost with remaining whipped cream to cover roll.
4. Chill 5 hours.

To serve, slice roll diagonally for a delicious striped cake.

23.

 Sweet Cereal Mix — Absolutely Irresistible

You will need: 9 cups square rice or wheat cereal
1 c. chocolate chips
1/4 c. margarine
1 1/2 c. powdered sugar

1. Melt chocolate and margarine (about 1 min.) in microwave. Stir.
2. In large bowl, pour melted chocolate over cereal. Mix until coated.
3. Put cereal in bag with powdered sugar. Shake to coat.
4. Spread onto wax paper to cool.

24.

Personal Cheese Pizzas — Your Very Own Pizza! Yummy!

You will need: flour tortilla
grated cheese

1. Spread cheese on tortilla.
2. Place in microwave 30 seconds until cheese melts.
3. Using pizza cutter, cut into 8 triangles.

25.

Applesauce Whip — A Delicious After-School Snack!

You will need: 1 cup applesauce
 ¼ cup raisins
 1 tsp. lemon juice
 1 cup whipped topping

1. Mix first 3 ingredients.
2. Spread jam in a circle on top of peanut butter.
3. Fold in whipped topping.

26.

Snow Cones

You will need: juice
 blender

1. Freeze juice in ice cube trays.
2. When frozen, put 3–6 cubes into blender. Turn blender on and off until cubes reach a snowy consistency.
3. Pour into a paper cup to serve.

27.

My Favorite Recipe

SHAKE, RATTLE AND ROLL

Here are the twelve most needed craft recipes.

Whether it be for school projects or fun at home, if you have kids you can't be without this section.

Copy recipes onto cardstock, cut out and laminate and place in your recipe file box.

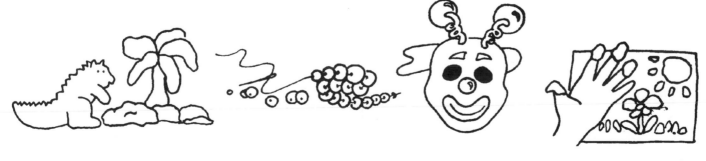

SHAKE, RATTLE AND ROLL

1. Dish Soap Bubbles
2. Kitchen Clay
3. Play Dough
4. Oblique
5. Salt Beads
6. Papier Mâché Flour Paste
7. Sticker Stuff
8. Salt Dough
9. Liquid Starch Fingerpaint
10. Moldable Soap
11. Corn Starch Modeling Clay
12. Stain Glass Paint

1.

Dish Soap Bubbles — For the Biggest, Longest-Lasting Bubbles

You will need: 1 cup dish soap
10 cups water

For longer-lasting bubbles add either 1/4 cup glycerin (located by hand lotion at pharmacy) or 1/4 cup vegetable oil and 1 tbsp. alcohol.

2.

Kitchen Clay — Moldable Clay That Hardens into the Shapes You Make

You will need: 2 cups baking soda
1 cup corn starch
1 1/2 cups cold water

Blend soda and starch. Add water, blend until smooth. Cook to boiling on medium heat. Stir constantly. Cook 1 more minute.

When clay is cool, mold into shapes you want. Let dry. Can be sanded. Can also be coated with clear shellac.

3.

Play Dough — Soft Dough That Never Crumbles

You will need: 1 c. flour
2 tsp. cream of tartar
1 tbsp. oil
1 c. water
food coloring

Mix first five ingredients in pan. Stir over medium heat until mixture thickens. Drop in food coloring and mix. Can be stored for months.

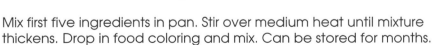

4.

Oblique — The Funniest Mixture You Have Ever Seen!
It Looks Watery But Cracks
Kids Can Play with This Stuff for Hours!

You will need: $1/2$ cup corn starch
$1/4$ cup water

1. Pour corn starch into bowl.
2. Slowly add water while stirring.
3. Add food coloring, if desired.

5.

Salt Beads — Make Necklaces with Your Own Handmade Beads

You will need: $1/2$ cup salt
$1/4$ cup corn starch
$1/4$ cup water
1 tsp. food coloring

1. Heat salt in water until very hot.
2. Add salt water to other ingredients.
3. Knead until smooth.
4. Pinch off small amount, roll into balls. Slide a toothpick through

6.

Papier Mâché Flour Paste —
Great for Masks, Piñatas, and Lots of Other Crafts

You will need: flour
water

1. Mix flour and water to form a watery glue-like substance.
2. Dip strands of newspaper into mixture, wipe off slightly and place onto object, or spread directly onto object with paintbrush.
3. Cover object with paper dipped in flour paste, then let dry. Repeat 2 times for best results.

7.

Sticker Stuff — Make Your Very Own Stickers!

You will need: paper
                pens, crayons
                1 pkg. gelatin

1. Color paper with pens and crayons in the designs you want for your stickers.
2. Make gelatin according to directions on package. Let cool slightly.
3. With paintbrush, spread gelatin onto back of decorated paper.
4. Let dry.
   To use, simply moisten gelatin and stick on. You can even try flavored gelatin for a yummy taste.

8.

Salt Dough — Make Ornaments, Beads, or Special Pottery

You will need: 2 cups flour
                1 cup salt
                1 cup water

1. Mix flour and salt in large bowl.
2. *Slowly* add water a little bit at a time. Mix as you pour to form a ball (not sticky).
3. Knead mixture 7-10 min. until smooth and firm.
4. Mold into shapes and bake at 325° F for 1 hour (or longer) to harden (or leave out for 1-2 days). Dough will keep 5 days in a plastic bag.

9.

Liquid Starch Fingerpaint — Every Kid Will Love This One!

You will need: 1 c. liquid starch
                poster paint

1. Pour liquid starch on a wet surface until desired color and consistency.
2. While stirring, slowly add paint.

10.

Moldable Soap —
Make Your Own Fun Soaps in Every Shape and Fragrance!
Great for Gifts.

You will need: soap flakes
water
fragrances, if desired

1. Pour a handful of soap flakes into a bowl.
2. Add water, a few drops at a time until it feels like soft clay.
3. Mold into desired shapes — hearts, flowers, or snowmen.
4. You can add scents by purchasing fragrance oil at the pharmacy.

11.

Corn Starch Modeling Clay — A Stiff Dough to Shape and Mold

You will need: 1 cup corn starch
1 1/2 cup flour
1 cup salt
warm water

1. Sift together dry ingredients.
2. Slowly add warm water until a stiff dough forms. Color can be added with water.
3. Model into desired shapes.
4. Let dry.
5. Paint, if desired.

12.

Stained Glass Paint

You will need: 1/2 cup corn syrup
food coloring

1. Mix food coloring into corn syrup until desired color is obtained.
2. Paint picture on paper.
3. Let dry several days before hanging.

Kids

AND THEIR

Organizing Everything!

Table of Contents

Introduction

Along with the wondrous joy of children comes the reality of an occasional mess or two. It seems like a continual challenge to help children keep their rooms clean.

It is important to be patient with children and to remember not to dwell too much on having a picture-perfect home. Children need to be free to decorate their rooms their way and display their treasures and creations.

Although we may never find a magic trick to keep the house perfectly clean, hopefully the ideas in this chapter will help you and your children in the struggle for cleanliness and order in their rooms and the bathroom.

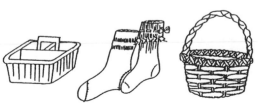

Kids
AND THEIR CLUTTER

Do you ever have a problem
with keeping your house neat?
You work and slave all day long
but end up in defeat?
You really try your hardest
You never seem to stop,
You clean, you wash you polish,
and pick up 'til you drop —
But then you get back up,
You tidy things some more
And just when things are looking good
something spills all over the floor.
So once again you wipe and scrub
And once more you mop and sweep,
Your smile slowly begins to fade
and your eyes begin to weep.
You think you are a failure
You've tried everything you know,
But wait, there's a method guaranteed
to work every time and so —
Here is your solution
for a house clean to the core —
Just hire a maid, a butler and cook
and send the kids next door.

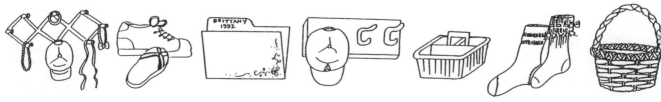

140

File Folders

An area for file folders is a must for every family. Whether you purchase a filing cabinet or get an old box, this is the first item in an organized home.

Children are usually going in a million different directions — so keep track of everything by creating a file system.

Some ideas for your file folders are:
- School information, PTA
- Soccer, baseball, basketball
- Birth certificates
- Immunization records
- Report cards
- Dentist, orthodontist, eye doctor
- Health club or recreation center
- Lessons — dance, voice, music
- Instructions for games
- Warranties for toys
- Social Security number information

Keep information that you need frequently in folders close to your telephone. Rarely needed Information can be stored in a filing cabinet in an office or garage.

Personal Files

A great idea for keeping track of children's important papers, awards, photos, and letters is to make a file folder for each child.

1. Label file with name and year (tape edges so small items won't be lost).

2. Let child decorate and personalize it.

3. Fill with special papers and pictures.

4. At the end of the year, they have a collection of their valuable treasures — to be saved in their special box or placed in a scrapbook.

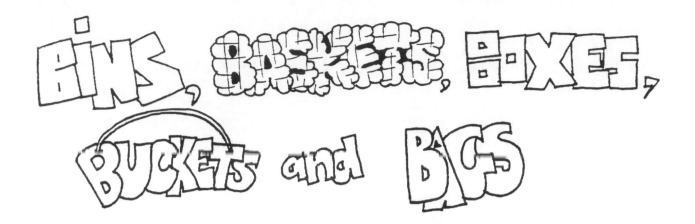

Bins

Children need to have a place to keep things. A small investment in some storage units can fulfill this need and make life easier for everyone. Bins come in a wide variety of sizes and colors, are fairly inexpensive, and quite durable. Small stackable bins are great for erasers, marbles, jacks, buttons, and guitar picks. Larger ones are perfect for balls, dolls, mitts, scarves, and even clothes.

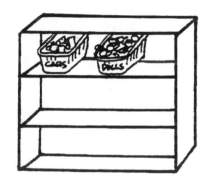

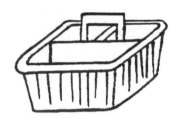

Plastic-handled bins are wonderful for keeping similar items together. They can be labeled with model paint and are easily accessible. Some great uses for bins are:

Hair Supplies — brushes, combs, hair spray, barrettes, curlers, bobby pins, and squirt bottles.

Art Supplies — crayons, paints, pencils, glue, glitter, paper, and chalk.

First Aid Kit — Bandages, ointment, aspirin, and petroleum jelly.

Make-Up (for older girls) — she can keep the bin in her room and carry make-up to the bathroom.

Cleaning items — sponges, cleaners, rags, and paper towels.

Toys — small books, puzzles, tapes — great for taking to grandma's house or on a long drive.

Baskets

Baskets are another great organization tool. Plastic baskets are made in numerous sizes and shapes. Baskets make drawer clutter almost non-existent. There are baskets made shallow enough to fit in desk drawers or deep enough to store dirty clothes. Brightly colored baskets set on shelves look cheerful while facilitating easy clean-up.

Buckets

Large buckets are great for storing children's toys. They are easily carried and very durable. Buckets are especially good for wooden or plastic blocks, cars, action figures, and balls. Bulk laundry detergent often comes in a bucket container with a lid. Buckets can be decorated and labeled with model paint.

Bags

How could one possibly think of organizing a child's room without sealable bags? Small ones are perfect for hair barrettes, doll clothes, or small cars. Larger ones can be filled with puzzles, headbands, school supplies, and small games. Once items are sorted into bags, they can be put into a box for safe-keeping and easy playing.

Boxes

Boxes are another wonderful item for organizing. They are made in every size imaginable and also come in beautifully decorated patterns to match any room. Particularly useful are under-the-bed boxes which children can reach with ease. Plastic shoe boxes are very durable and stack nicely on top of each other. These are especially good for things such as cards, markers, and stickers.

Special Box

One of the most important items in a child's room is the child's "special" box. This is a necessity for every child. Children love to save everything, which can create an inordinate amount of clutter. When they have a place for their most prized possessions, they begin to differentiate what is really important and what is not. The special box is the place for important valentines, old ticket stubs, beautiful rocks, and leaves that are too wonderful to throw away.

The special box should be placed in an area that is easily reached so the child can go through it at any time. Not only is this an excellent way to keep memories alive, but it is a wonderful way for children to reaffirm who they are.

Storage Boxes

Every family needs boxes for storage. Look through your child's room and see what could be stored to eliminate clutter. When summer is over, store swimsuits, beach towels, and sunscreen. After winter, store mittens, hats, and boots. Storage boxes are great for seldom-used items, keepsakes, and children's projects. Use the following storage system to keep track of every item you store:

1. Label each box with a large number.

2. List items in each box on storage box sheet (see next page) and store in a file folder or notebook, or use a recipe card file.

3. Refer to your list with the corresponding number to locate items.

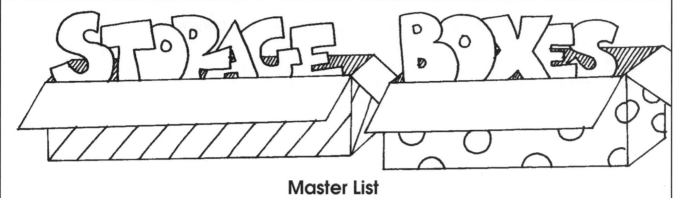

Master List

How to Keep a Child's Room Clean

There are several things parents can do to help their children have tidy rooms. First, a parent must always remember that the ability to clean up a room is a skill that takes time and effort to develop. Children should gradually be taught how to keep their rooms clean.

The second thing a parent must do is to make the room easy to keep clean. Here are some ideas to make the job easier.

A child must have a designated place for dirty laundry. A colorful wastebasket or an old pillowcase hung in the closet does a great job. There are several commercial items available that are also fun ideas for dirty clothes.

Closets should be made so that children can reach them. If possible, place closet clothes bar at children's level. If this is not possible, a good step stool will help.

Children should have ample hangers that are the right size for their clothes. Hangers that are too large are difficult for children to use and can stretch clothes out of shape. Colorful plastic hangers are available and are much easier for children to use than the wire variety.

Make sure children have adequate closet and drawer space. When drawers are overflowing, it is difficult for children to put away clothes.

Parents' Checklist for a Child's Room

As parents, we sometimes need to step back and view life from a child's perspective. Look at your child's room and see if it is manageable.

- Is there a place for trash?
- Is there a laundry hamper?
- Can child reach closet bar?
- Are there clothes that are not worn taking up space (too old or too small)?
- Is there a bulletin board?
- Is there a special box?

- Can child easily make the bed?
- Is there a place for everything?
- Are there too many toys?
- Are dresser drawers easily opened and not too full?
- Are pictures and shelves hung at a child's level?
- Are toys easily stored?

CLOTHES & BOWS etc...

Grosgrain Ribbon Holder

1. Take $^3/4$" tucks every 3" on ribbon.
2. Insert bows inside the tucks to hold and keep from sliding.
3. Hang over hook or decorative nail.

Hats

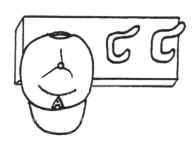

- Hooks are wonderful for hanging hats.
- Cup racks hold many hats and can be very inexpensive.
- Hats can be used to decorate a child's room by hanging them on nails around the top of the wall. This is great for baseball hat collections.

Braided Yarn Bow Holder

1. Get several strands of yarn 1 yard long.
2. Tie yarn together and braid. Secure at bottom.
3. Hair bows and barrettes can be easily attached through or around braided yarn.

Stuffed Animals

- Nets can be purchased to hang high in the corner of a room to keep stuffed animals neat.
- A shelf can be placed at the top of a wall in a child's room to hold stuffed animals — a cute border decoration.
- A long piece of Velcro® can be attached to a wall and smaller opposing pieces attached to animals — they can be stored out of the way and easily used.

Shoes

Try having children remove shoes before they enter the house. Shoes will not get lost and the carpet will stay cleaner.

A shoe shelf in the closet keeps shoes orderly and neat. Bins are great for tennis shoes, slippers, and sandals.

Plastic shoe boxes are wonderful to keep shoes neat and organized — they stack easily to make more closet space.

Socks

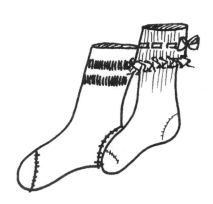

Plastic bins are great for storing socks in the closet.

Mark each sock on the toe with a permanent marker for easy matching. Use a different color or shape for each child.

Shoe boxes are great drawer organizers for socks and underwear.

Collections

Kids like to collect things, but collections can often become clutter. Find a good storage area to keep items neat and organized.

Small items like rocks, keys, seashells, thimbles, balloons, and coins can be stored in:
- an embroidery floss container
- a baby food box
- a nail organizer

Flat items like baseball cards, post cards, stickers, and postage stamps can be placed in notebooks with plastic folders for storage or stacked neatly in shoe boxes.

Large collections like teddy bears or dolls can be stored in a large box and rotated.

Fragile collections need to be placed on a high shelf to eliminate risk of anything being broken.

Clothespin Hanger

A clever way to display art, homework, and posters, or to hold ribbons and hats is to make a clothespin hanger.

1. Glue cute wooden shapes onto clothespins (purchase at a craft store).
2. Glue clothespins onto board with the pinching end pointed down.
3. Mount to wall.

Bulletin Boards

A family bulletin board is a must for every home with children. Each month, display their art projects, awards, and special school work. At the end of the month, clear it off and allow children to put these items in their special boxes.

It is important for children to have bulletin boards in their rooms to display their own personal items.

Hooks

Hooks are very important for a child in keeping a clean room.

Cup racks may be purchased, usually inexpensively. They are great for jewelry, hair ribbons, belts, hats, and coats.

Also available are boards with hooks and pegs on them. They are more difficult to find and are usually more expensive.

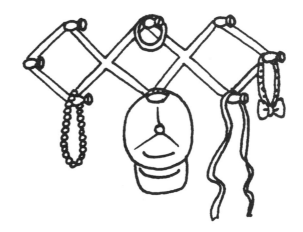

Nail Organizers

Great for jewelry and marbles, rubber bands, safety pins, nail clippers, thumb tacks, small toys, batteries, and odds-and-ends. Label the drawers with model paint.

Embroidery Floss or Fishing Tackle Box

Great for barrettes, small toys, collections, doll accessories, erasers, and stickers. Use model paint to label each compartment with the name of the item that should be stored in the compartment.

Lockers

Lockers are wonderful for a child's room or garage. They can be purchased at home supply stores or they can be easily made.

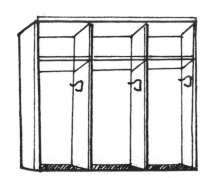

1. Make or purchase wood shelving (as shown).

2. Line bottom with carpet remnants for shoes.

3. Place hooks on back and sides to hold backpacks and jackets.

4. Shelves on top are perfect for books and homework.

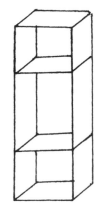

Bins can be stacked to resemble a locker as well.

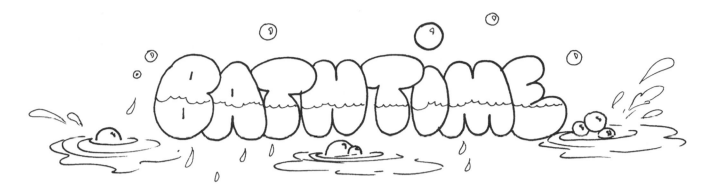

Children enjoy bathtime. They can relax, pretend, and have a wonderful time playing in bubbly water. But when the bath is over, the mess can be overwhelming.

Following are some ideas to make bathtime fun for kids and easier on everyone else:

Bathroom Helps

- Make sure each bathroom has a laundry basket for dirty clothes.

- A small step-stool helps children use the sink. This cuts down the amount of mess to be cleaned up.

- Small disposable paper cups allow children to get their own drinks.

- Small toothpaste tubes are easier for children. Show them how to roll up the end so toothpaste mess is cut down. Flip-caps and new pump dispensers are also wonderful for children.

- Bath items can be stored and easily seen using a clear vinyl shoebag hung on a closet door. Kids can quickly find cotton swabs, bandages, and brushes.

- Always supervise small children. Many little ones drown each year in the bath.

- Make sure the bottom of your tub has a no-slip surface or purchase one to eliminate accidents in the tub.

Dishpan

A dishpan is a great way to store tub toys. When a child is done with his or her bath, have the child put the toys in the dishpan. They will dry off and be ready for the next bath.

Mesh Bag

Another handy way to keep tub toys from making a mess is to make a net bag with a drawstring closure. Then hang the bag from the tub faucet. Dish towels can be used instead of net.

Towel Hooks

To cut down the number of dirty towels a family goes through each week, simply hang a hook in a closet or behind the bathroom door for each child to hang his towel. Large cup racks work well if you need many hooks.

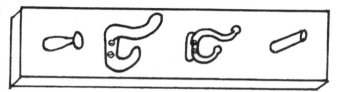

Personal Towels

Another idea is to give each child his or her own special towel. Buy their favorite color towel and let them personalize it by decorating with lace or ribbon.

Timer

A small timer set near the tub is a perfect way for children to know when it is time to "get out!" This is especially good for older children who like to take long showers.

Soap

Bar soaps were not meant for small hands. They are difficult enough for adults to handle, let alone kids. Purchasing small soaps can be very helpful for young children. Hotel soap bars are the perfect size, too.

Soap In A Bag

Soap bars can be put in a small, mesh drawstring bag. They can be used without removing them from the bag, then hung up from the tub faucet. Make sure tubs have a plastic soap dish so soap won't dissolve while sitting on the bottom of the tub.

Squeeze Bottles

Shampoo containers can be very difficult for small hands. An alternative is to purchase small squeeze bottles and fill them with shampoo or bubble bath. Pump bottles also work well. Bottles can be labeled with model paint.

Bath Mitt

A bath mitt is a fun way to get children clean! Use the pattern on the next page to form a mitten out of two washcloths. Personalize with trim or fabric paint.

Wrap-around Towel

A cozy idea for keeping children dry when they get out of the tub is to make a wrap-around towel. Sew Velcro® onto towel as shown and you have an instant cover-up! The towel can be wrapped around the chest or waist.

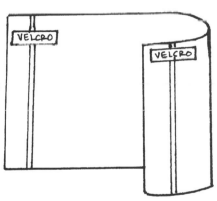

Sponges

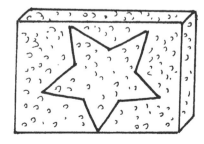

Sponges are a great tub toy. For extra fun, cut different colored sponges into a variety of cute shapes. Compressed sponge material can be purchased at craft stores to make cutting easier. Shapes will expand into sponges after soaking in water.

Plastic Holder

A plastic holder with handles is great for storing bath items for baby. Fill with baby shampoo, baby powder, and washcloths to make baby's bathtime easier.

Pattern for Bath Mitt

kids' steps

Reading, Writing, and Relating to Your Child's Education

kids' steps

Table of Contents

kids' steps

Introduction

Kids' Steps is a collection of ideas to help you survive your child's education.

It is important to be involved in your child's school. Join the PTA, volunteer to help in the classroom, or just offer your support in a way suitable to your family's needs. Do get to know your child's teacher. If there are problems or concerns, work together with the teacher and principal to find a solution. They want to know and are eager to help.

Reading is such an important skill in our society that several ideas are presented to help children read. Suggested book lists are given for each of the first three grades to help parents or grandparents in selecting appropriate books for their young children.

kids' steps

Why do we have to go to school,
Can't we stay home just for once?
All we do is work, work, work
For months and months and months.

Who was it that invented school
Where we have to sit all day?
Someone was trying to punish kids
Because we want to go out to play.

I'm so excited class is out,
School is such a bore.
Except for Art, P.E., and recess
The rest is just a chore.

When Mom says, "How did it go today?"
I just reply, "Not bad."
But a B in English is pretty good,
And my science experiment was rad!

When Dad says, "What happened today?"
I always tell him, "Nothing."
Well, I read a book and learned new math,
I guess that is something.

When Grandma asks, "What did you learn?"
I can't think of anything to say.
But we learned about space and how things grow,
And a lot about the USA.

Mrs. Johnson is okay I guess,
She says I'm pretty awesome.
Even if I flunk a test
She doesn't think I'm dumb.

My friends always say school is a drag,
And I usually agree.
But when I'm alone, I must admit
It's not that bad to me.

Even though I fuss and moan,
When all is said and done,
I'm glad I have to go to school,
It's really pretty fun.

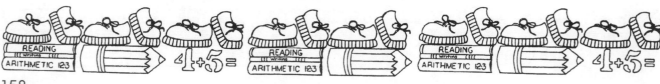

100 Ways to Say Good Job!

Kids can never hear "Good job!" enough! Below is a list of 100 ways to praise your child. For a great self-esteem booster, try saying the whole list to your child in one day.

On the following page you will find cards that send the "Good job!" message through an extra special compliment. Copy, color, and cut out. Leave in lunch sack, at the breakfast table, or on a pillow.

1. SUPER GOOD!
2. You've got it made.
3. Now you've figured it out.
4. That's RIGHT!
5. FANTASTIC!
6. You're really working hard today.
7. You are very good at that.
8. That's coming along nicely.
9. GOOD WORK!
10. That's very much better.
11. I'm happy to see you're working like that!
12. Exactly right.
13. I'm proud of the way you worked today.
14. You are doing that much better today.
15. You've just about got it.
16. That's the best you have ever done.
17. You're doing a good job!
18. THAT'S IT!
19. Right on!
20. That's quite an improvement.
21. GREAT!
22. I knew you could do it.
23. Congratulations!
24. Not bad.
25. Great effort.
26. Now you have it.
27. You are learning fast.
28. Good for you!
29. Couldn't have done it better myself.
30. BEAUTIFUL!
31. One more time and you'll have it.
32. You really make my job fun.
33. That's the right way to do it.
34. You're getting better every day.
35. You did it that time!
36. You're on the right track now.
37. Nice going.
38. You haven't missed a thing.
39. WOW!
40. That's the way.
41. Keep up the good work.
42. TERRIFIC!
43. Nothing can stop you now.
44. That's the way to do it.
45. SENSATIONAL!
46. You've got your brain in gear today.
47. You are very talented.
48. EXCELLENT!
49. That was first-class work.
50. That's the best ever.
51. You've just about mastered that.
52. PERFECT!
53. That's better than ever!
54. Much better!
55. WONDERFUL!
56. You must have been practicing!
57. You did that very well.
58. FINE!
59. You are a pleasure to work with.
60. You're really going to town.
61. OUTSTANDING!
62. That's good.
63. TREMENDOUS!
64. That's how to handle that!
65. Now that's what I call a fine job.
66. That's unbelievable.
67. SUPER!
68. You're really improving!
69. You're doing beautifully.
70. Superb!
71. Good remembering!
72. You've got that down pat.
73. You certainly did well today.
74. Keep it up!
75. Kudos!
76. You did a lot of work today.
77. Well, look at you go!
78. You are amazing.
79. I'm very proud of you!
80. I like that.
81. MARVELOUS!
82. Way to go!
83. Now you have the hang of it!
84. You're doing fine.
85. Good thinking.
86. You are really learning a lot.
87. Good going.
88. I've never seen you do it better.
89. Keep on trying!
90. You outdid yourself today!
91. What high quality work!
92. I think you've got it now.
93. That's a good boy/girl.
94. Good job!
95. You figured that out fast.
96. You remembered!
97. That's really nice.
98. That kind of work makes me happy.
99. I can't believe you are this good!
100. Awesome!

159

How to be Actively Involved in Your Child's Education

1. Display your child's school work and keep a file or box of special achievements and projects.

2. Attend parent-teacher conferences, PTA meetings, and other programs and activities at your school.

3. See that their homework is completed each night. Make sure your children have a quiet place to study and proper supplies and materials to complete their work.

4. Ask your children what they learned in school. Show genuine interest and be available to help with any homework.

5. Have a positive attitude toward education, teachers, and school policies. Let children know education is an important part of life.

6. Be positive about their experiences at school and they will be pleased to share their school day with you.

7. Volunteer to help in the classroom. Most teachers love all the help they can get.

8. Make sure your child has free time to play and have fun. Don't have all out-of-school hours be filled with activity.

9. Encourage children to do their best without putting pressure on them to be the best!

10. Be a good example. Show your child that you value education in your own life and in the lives of your children.

What Teachers Want Parents to Know

1. Be involved in your child's education. Volunteer, support projects, and attend activities.

2. Emphasize academics, not extra-curricular activities and athletics.

3. Encourage children to do their best, but don't put excessive pressure to excel above others.

4. Call teachers if you are uncomfortable about a situation or if you suspect a problem.

5. Accept parental responsibility. Teachers are there to support parents, not be the parent.

6. Support school rules and goals, and take an active role in establishing school policies and procedures.

7. Set a good example. Habits formed in the home set the atmosphere for learning and create a desire for education.

Ten Ways to Increase Learning in the Classroom

Take a few minutes of your time to remind your child of these few activities, attitudes, and behaviors that can increase learning:

1. Pay close attention in class.

2. Don't put off assignments. Do them right away.

3. Make every effort to learn to effectively use reference materials, such as dictionaries, encyclopedias, and atlases.

4. Read as much as possible — anything and everything.

5. Visit the library often.

6. Always ask questions if an assignment is not clear.

7. Set aside time for study each day in a quiet, well-lighted area.

8. Ask for help only when really necessary. Too much help will hinder learning.

9. Always check over completed work. Catching mistakes before handing in assignments may lead to better grades.

10. Eat right, stay in shape, and get plenty of rest.

Parent Evaluation Checklist

___ 1. Do you answer your child's questions with patience and good humor?

___ 2. Do you take advantage of their questions and expressions of interest to guide them into further learning and exploration?

___ 3. Do you help them develop physical and social skills as carefully as you encourage mental growth?

___ 4. Do you encourage your child to get along with other children of all levels of intelligence and ability?

___ 5. Do you set reasonable standards of behavior for your children and then see that they meet them?

___ 6. Do you impose firm and fair discipline that is neither too harsh nor too permissive?

___ 7. Do you show them they are admired by you?

___ 8. Do you try to find something specific to praise when shown their work?

___ 9. Do you suggest worthwhile reading materials and television programs?

___ 10. Do you provide places where they can display their work?

___ 11. Do you participate in some of their activities?

___ 12. Do you let them learn about and share in some of your hobbies and interests?

___ 13. Do you teach them how to budget time, organize work, and improve study habits?

___ 14. Do you help them make their own plans and decisions?

___ 15. Do you avoid overemphasizing intellectual achievement?

___ 16. Do you teach them to use their gifts for the benefit of society, rather than for themselves only?

___ 17. Will your expressions of attitude and your behavior set the example you want them to follow?

___ 18. Will you avoid talking down to them?

___ 19. Will you speak as properly as you want them to?

Ten Ways to Encourage Reading

1. **Start early. Read a lot.**

   Read to your children — cards, signs, letters, newspapers. They need to hear what it sounds like to read.

2. **Introduce books early.**

   Start with simple picture books and progress as a child develops. Children enjoy the pictures and begin to develop a love of reading.

3. **Visit the library often.**

   Let children pick their own books, but help them to find books that might be of special interest to them or of appropriate difficulty.

4. **Have a regular storytime.**

   A regular time for reading is a great activity for children. Whether it is bedtime, naptime, or before dinner, a routine of reading will be anticipated and enjoyed by children.

5. **Be an example.**

   Let your children see you read! Talk about what you are reading. This stimulates a strong desire to be able to read well.

6. **Give books and children's magazine subscriptions as gifts.**

   Children will value these books and understand that reading is important.

7. **Have children read to you.**

   Let them read to you while you are cooking, weeding, or painting. They will enjoy it and you can help when needed.

8. **Keep a lot of reading material in your home.**

   Keep children's books easily available to them.

9. **Limit television, computer games, and movies.**

   Don't let television become a habit or a babysitter.

10. **Make it fun.**

    If a child does not appear interested, try another book or another time. Keep in mind the age and attention span of each child.

Preschool

Preschool

More and more parents are opting to place their children in preschools to help them be prepared for kindergarten.

The most crucial decision regarding preschool is picking the right one. Several suggestions for selecting preschools can be found in the Family Safety chapter. These should help you feel comfortable about where your children will spend their time. Take a few minutes to review these ideas so you can be at ease with your decision.

To help you deal with your preschooler, some general characteristics are given on the following page for children 1 to 4 years old. In this chapter, you will also find some ideas and several resources to help prepare your preschooler to read.

Preschooler Characteristics

When dealing with very small children, it is helpful to understand where they are developmentally. The following is a brief generalization of characteristics of young children.

1 – 1 1/2 Years Old

Children reaching the age of one can crawl and are usually beginning to walk, run, and climb. Their coordination is not very developed and they get tired very easily. They are beginning to speak, with two of their most common words being "mine" and "no." Children this age love short stories, but their attention span is quite short. They cry very easily and sharing is nearly impossible.

2 Years Old

Toddlers reaching the age of two are very active. They can run, jump, and get into everything. Their attention span is about two to three minutes long, so activities need to be short and varied. Two-year-olds are very curious and enjoy doing things over and over again. Sharing and cooperating are extremely difficult. They usually respond well to physical contact. They like to be in close proximity to adults. They are very emotional and like to be independent.

3 – 4 Years Old

Three-year-olds can walk, run, kick, and climb. Their small muscle development is not as advanced as their larger muscle coordination. These children love to pretend, are very imaginative, curious, and inquisitive. Sharing is still difficult, but they are beginning to be able to play with friends. Three-year-olds thrive on approval, love, and praise from adults. They are becoming more independent.

Ten Attention-Getters for Children

1. Try starting your question or comment by using the child's name.

2. Use eye-to-eye contact while talking, and talk at child's level, if possible.

3. A gentle touch on the shoulder or hand can bring a child's attention to you.

4. Change tone or volume of your voice.

5. Create a code word or sign that means, "I need your attention."

6. Use a puppet to tell the child what he or she must do.

7. Turn lights off and on.

8. Use a ball or beanbag. Throw it to the child and let him or her throw it back when he or she makes the proper response.

9. Sing directions to young children. Make up songs they can sing with you.

10. Snap fingers or clap hands to a beat. Have them copy you. When they are with you, fold hands and give your comment.

Tips for Reading Aloud

Reading aloud is an important step in learning to read. The following tips may be helpful as you read to your child.

1. Set a good mood. Don't make a child dread storytime by being harsh. Let the atmosphere suggest a quiet and cozy time for reading.

2. Use expression. Try changing your voice for different characters. Become loud or soft, slow or fast, depending on the character or situation. This will bring life to the story.

3. Challenge your child's mind. Find books that are stimulating to your child.

4. Pace. Don't race through a book. Find a book that is the right length for the amount of time you have.

5. Patience. Allow children to ask questions. If they are curious, they are interested.

Some good books on reading aloud are:

FOR READING OUT LOUD, A Guide to Sharing Books with Children. Margaret M. Kimmel and Elizabeth Segar.

THE READ-ALOUD HANDBOOK. Jim Trelease.

CLASSICS TO READ ALOUD TO YOUR CHILDREN. William F. Russell.

Getting Ready to Read

The following list of resources is meant to help parents introduce books to their preschool children and to prepare the children for learning to read.

• **Reading to Babies and Preschoolers**

BABIES NEED BOOKS, Butler, Dorothy.

GETTING READY TO READ, Boegehold, Betty.
This practical guide for parents describes pre-reading learning activities designed to enhance language development, listening skills, and a love of books.

RAISING READERS: A Guide to Sharing Literature with Young Children. National Council of Teachers of English. How parents can help children become readers — starting with infants. Annotated book lists are included by age groups, plus children's magazines and publishers are listed in the appendices.

READ TO ME! TEACH ME!, Rossi, Mary Jane.
Discussion of the types of books appropriate for particular ages and recommended titles.

READING BEGINS AT HOME, Butler, Dorothy.
Preparing children for reading before they go to school.

• **Reading at Elementary Ages**

CHOOSING BOOKS FOR KIDS, Oppenheim, Joanne.
A companion volume to *GETTING READY TO READ* with year-by-year child development and how that affects what a child will read, plus reviews of books for babies to young adults.

GROWING UP READING, Lamme, Linda.

GROWING UP WRITING, Lamme, Linda.
Together these two books give parents hundreds of ideas for learning activities that help children learn naturally to read and write.

HELP YOUR CHILD TO READ BETTER, Schiavone, James.
Describes the reading process, special problems, and developmental stages for preschoolers, elementary-age children, and teenagers, plus suggestions for parents on working with their children in developing better reading skills.

MAKE YOUR CHILD A LIFELONG READER, Gross, Jacquelyn. A parent-guided program for children of all ages.

• Reading at Elementary Ages (cont'd.)

ON LEARNING TO READ, Bettelheim, Bruno.
A world-renowned psychologist presents a strong case for teaching the love of reading rather than mere skill in decoding words.

• Determining Quality in Children's Books

CHOOSING BOOKS FOR CHILDREN: A Common Sense Guide, Hearne, Betsy.
Witty and perceptive, Hearne's book is designed to provide guidelines for choosing high-quality children's books and stresses sharing book experiences from infancy to early teens. A selection of some of her favorite books for various ages is included.

GOOD BOOKS TO GROW ON, Cascardi, Andrea.
A guide to the best books for babies to five-year-olds organized by developmental stages, with ideas on where to find more good books through book clubs, mail order services, magazines, and specialty bookstores.

HOW TO CHOOSE GOOD BOOKS FOR KIDS, McMullan, Kate.
Criteria for different age groups, hints for motivating reluctant readers, and finding that special book your child will treasure.

• Reading Readiness Activities

ART, BOOKS AND CHILDREN, Frost, Joan.
Art activities based on children's literature.

CREATIVE ENCOUNTERS, Polkingham, Anne.
Activities to expand children's responses to literature.

GAMES FOR READING: Playful Ways to Help Your Child Read, Kaye, Peggy.
Games for learning words, sounds, understanding, and reading.

USING LITERATURE WITH YOUNG CHILDREN, 2nd Ed., Coody, Betty.
Books that lead to art, cooking, drama, and language experiences, plus activities for children from one to eight years of age.

BASIC BEGINNINGS: A Handbook of Learning Games, Kirchner, Audrey.
Game and activity patterns for four- to six-year-olds that develop basic pre-reading skills, such as sequencing, visual perception, basic math, and language experiences.

CREATIVE ACTIVITIES FOR YOUNG CHILDREN, Chenfeld, Mimi.
Activities include hand- and foot-prints, musical instruments to express feelings, songs of welcome and hospitality, floor shapes, and field trips.

EXPLORE AND CREATE, Hibner, Dixie, ed.
Art, games, cooking, and science, plus activities for young children.

I CAN DO IT! I CAN DO IT!, Gilbert, LaBritta.
135 successful independent learning activities for preschoolers, ranging from color sticks to puzzles to ABCs and numbers.

- **Reading Readiness Activities (cont'd.)**

  CRAFTS, Warren, Jean.
  Activities and ideas to use with young children that develop skills in language, science, and math.

  LEARNING THROUGH ALL FIVE SENSES, McCue, Lois.
  A language development activity book.

  LOOK AT ME: Activities for Babies and Toddlers, Haas, Carolyn.
  Hundreds of concrete ideas and projects organized according to developmental levels that promote parental interactions with young children for the mutual benefit of both.

  OPEN THE DOORS LET'S EXPLORE, Redleaf, Rhoda.
  Neighborhood field trips for young children with follow-up activities.

  PLEASE TOUCH: HOW TO STIMULATE YOUR CHILD'S CREATIVE DEVELOPMENT THROUGH MOVEMENT, MUSIC, ART AND PLAY, Striker, Susan.
  Developmental skills, home environment, excursions, toys, art experiences, movement, and music are described for each age level from birth through four years.

  THINGS TO DO WITH TODDLERS AND TWOS, Miller, Karen.
  Hundreds of ideas for activities and toys that appeal to children one and two years old.

  RECIPES FOR ART AND CRAFT MATERIALS, Sattler, Helen.
  How to make home-made leather glue, finger-paint, paste, flower preservatives, play dough, etc., from common household ingredients.

  BIG BOOK OF RECIPES FOR FUN: Creative Learning Activities for Home and School, Haas, Carolyn.

  RECIPES FOR FUN AND LEARNING: Creative Learning Activities for Young Children, Haas, Carolyn.

  STILL MORE RECIPES FOR FUN, Cole, Ann.

- **Additional resources can be found at your local library under these subjects:**

  Finger Plays & Activities

  Craft Ideas

  Music Activities

  Music

  Storytelling

  Poetry

I Can Do

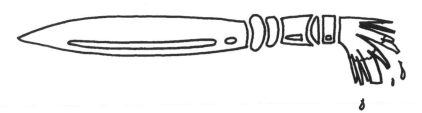

Kindergarten

Starting kindergarten is a very important step in a child's life! This section gives some information to help you make this year in your child's life successful.

- Characteristics of a kindergartner.

- Skills to help your child start kindergarten.

- Ten important developments during kindergarten.

- Teaching your child to print correctly.

- Sight words.

- Words and concepts for kindergarten.

Characteristics of a Kindergartner

Children, ages four and five, often exhibit some very similar characteristics and needs. Although every kindergarten child is an individual who varies from all others, there are some general likenesses. All children:

1. Need security. They are dependent on the affections of the adults who are near them.

2. Live in a here-and-now world. Their chief interests are limited to their own immediate experiences.

3. Are fond of stories, whereby they gain information.

4. Need a school program which allows freedom of movement, frequent changes of activity, and yet follows a definite pattern.

5. Play and learn best with very small groups or one other child.

6. Are seeking to gain control of their large muscles. They like to run, hop, skip, and climb.

7. Are anxious to investigate, examine, and question.

8. Are people with their own abilities and problems.

Skills to Help Your Child Start Kindergarten

1. Able to count to ten.

2. Able to recognize and print one's first name.

3. Understands sizes.

4. Recognizes numbers to ten, primary colors, basic shapes.

5. Knows parents' names.

6. Knows one's address and phone number.

7. Knows different parts of one's body.

8. Able to follow simple directions.

9. Able to repeat short sentences.

10. Able to use scissors, crayons, and paste.

11. Able to run, jump, hop, throw a ball, clap hands.

12. Able to button, zip, and snap.

13. Plays and shares with other children.

14. Able to leave parents and work independently.

To help your kindergartner start school:

Make sure your child gets adequate rest and a healthy breakfast. Children should know basic rules of cleanliness and how to use the bathroom facilities by themselves. Clothing worn to school should be labeled and washable.

Ten Important Developments During Kindergarten

During kindergarten, a child should learn to:

1. Share materials.

2. Express himself creatively.

3. Work and play well with others.

4. Follow directions.

5. Develop initiative and orginality.

6. Plan and carry out an activity.

7. Find satisfaction in achievements.

8. Observe good health practices.

9. Obey safety rules.

10. Be responsible for completing work and putting away materials.

Teaching Your Child to Print Correctly

To help prepare your child for kindergarten, it is important that he or she knows the proper way to form letters. If your child wants to work on writing his name, please teach him to use the capital letter for the first letter of his name, followed by lower case letters.

Sight Words

As children begin to read, they will learn to sound out words. But there are many words which can be learned by sight to facilitate reading.

Below are some common and simple sight words. As your child begins to read, have him or her read through some of the words each day or put these words on flashcards and review them periodically.

a	by	one	when
as	go	two	very
I	us	had	been
if	we	out	them
an	the	day	from
it	not	she	there
be	all	our	would
on	but	get	which
in	can	was	come
of	has	how	then
so	see	put	what
is	you	who	make
to	and	that	know
he	for	with	much
no	her	will	here
at	him	this	said
up	are	your	their
do	any	have	three
me	his	they	girl
or	man	good	boy
my	did	some	were

Words and Concepts for Kindergarten

Here is a list of words and concepts that will be helpful for your child to know when entering kindergarten. Use these words often to help the child grasp their meaning.

1. Top
2. Through
3. Away from
4. Next to
5. Inside
6. Some, not many
7. Middle
8. Few
9. Furthest
10. Around
11. Over
12. Widest
13. Most
14. Between
15. Whole
16. Nearest
17. Second
18. Corner
19. Several
20. Behind
21. Row
22. Different
23. After
24. Almost
25. Half

26. Center
27. As many
28. Side
29. Beginning
30. Other
31. Alike
32. Not first or last
33. Never
34. Below
35. Match
36. Always
37. Medium-sized
38. Right
39. Forward
40. Zero
41. Above
42. Every
43. Separated
44. Left
45. Pair
46. Skip
47. Equal
48. In order
49. Third
50. Least

Reading Lists

It is sometimes difficult to know what books are interesting and appropriate for your child.

On the following pages are some ideas to help you choose books that your child will enjoy. Children enjoy being read to at an early age, so the suggested reading lists start with books for preschool children who will be read to, and goes through third grade.

By the time children reach fourth grade, they have usually developed specific interests and feel very confident choosing their own books. If you do need guidance in choosing a book for an older child, check with your local librarian.

Books For Infants to Age Three

THE BABY'S CATALOGUE, Ahlberg, Allan and Janet.
This beautifully illustrated book teaches simple words by listing them next to illustrations.

ANNO'S PEEKABOO, Anno, Mitsumasa.
Every other page is a pair of hands playing peekaboo with an animal or person on the next page.

WATCHING FOXES, Arnosky, Jim.
While their mother is away from the den, four little foxes play in the sunlight.

TEN, NINE, EIGHT, Bang, Molly.
A father puts his daughter to bed while counting the things in her room.

GOING TO BED BOOK, Boynton, Sandra.
A group of animals get ready for bed in a humorous fashion. See also *BUT NOT THE HIPPOPOTAMUS; MOO, BAA, LA LA LA; OPPOSITES; HORNS TO TOES.*

HUSH LITTLE BABY, Brandenburg, Aliki.
An illustrated version of the old Appalachian lullaby. See also *WELCOME LITTLE BABY.*

HAND RHYMES, Brown, Marc.
A collection of nursery rhymes with diagrams for accompanying finger plays.

THE RUNAWAY BUNNY, Brown, Margaret Wise.
A baby bunny tries to run away from home, but his mother always finds him. See also *GOODNIGHT MOON.*

THE BLANKET, Burningham, John.
The whole family looks for a lost blanket. See also Burningham's books about sounds: *CLUCK BAA; JANGLE TWANG; SLAM BANG.*

THE VERY HUNGRY CATERPILLAR, Carle, Eric.
The book follows the progress of a hungry little caterpillar as he eats his way through a varied and very large quantity of food until, full at last, he forms a cocoon around himself and goes to sleep.

THE BABY'S LAP BOOK, Chorao, Kay.
An anthology of familiar nursery rhymes. See also Charao's series: *KATE'S SNOWMAN; KATE'S BOX; KATE'S CAR.*

CLEAN-UP DAY, Duke, Kate.
A mother guinea pig and her child clean house. See also *BEDTIME; THE PLAYGROUND; WHAT BOUNCES.*

Books for Infants to Age Three (cont'd.)

LITTLE BOAT, Gay, Michael.
A boat that works hard to get its job done. See also *LITTLE PLANE; LITTLE TRUCK*.

WHERE'S SPOT? Hill, Eric.
A mother dog finds eight other animals hiding around the house before finding her own lost puppy.
See also *SPOT'S BIRTHDAY*.

BATHWATER'S HOT, Hughes, Shirley.
A little girl discovers that all things have an opposite. See also *NOISY; WHEN WE WENT TO THE PARK*.

I SEE, Isadora, Rachel.
A baby responds to all of the things she sees. See also *I HEAR*.

A NEW BABY AT KOKO BEAR'S HOUSE, Lansky, Vicki.
A practical parenting read-together book with sections for both children and their parents. See also
KOKO BEAR'S NEW BABYSITTER; KOKO BEAR'S NEW POTTY.

SAM'S CAR, Lindgren, Barbro.
One of a series of simple stories in which Sam loses something precious but regains it without too
many tears. See also *SAM'S COOKIE; SAM'S TEDDY BEAR*.

DAD'S BACK, Ormerod, Jan.
An inquisitive little baby manages to disrupt Daddy at whatever he's doing. See also *MESSY BABY;
READING; SLEEPING*.

SAY GOODNIGHT, Oxenbury, Helen.
Four babies have a busy day that wears them out. See also *TICKLE, TICKLE; CLAP HANDS; ALL
FALL DOWN*.

TOM AND PIPPO MAKE A MESS, Oxenbury, Helen.
Tom is not very successful when he tries to help his father paint a room and blames his toy monkey,
Pippo, for the mess. See also *TOM AND PIPPO READ A STORY; TOM AND PIPPO GO FOR A WALK;
TOM AND PIPPO AND THE WASHING MACHINE*.

PUPPY'S ABC, Piers, Helen.
Photographs of a puppy with objects beginning with each letter of the alphabet.

GOBBLE, GROWL, GRUNT, Spier, Peter.
Appealing animal pictures fill the pages of this book of animal sounds.

IT'S SNOWING, LITTLE RABBIT, Wabbes, Marie.
Little Rabbit makes a snow rabbit that looks just like her. See also *HAPPY BIRTHDAY, LITTLE RABBIT;
LITTLE RABBIT'S GARDEN; and GOODNIGHT LITTLE RABBIT*.

Books for Infants to Age Three (cont'd.)

MAX'S FIRST WORDS, Wells, Rosemary.
Ruby patiently tries to teach her baby brother, Max, the correct words for various objects, but Max calls everything Bang, until Rudy shows him an apple. See also many other Max books such as *MAX'S RIDE; MAX'S NEW SUIT.*

MY HOUSE, Wilmer, Diane.
A boy invites us to his house to meet his parents, his sister and brother, and their pets. See also *DAYTIME; SHOPPING; NIGHTIME.*

THE LULLABY SONGBOOK, Yolen, Jane.
A collection of fifteen lullabies, each with an historic note and a musical arrangement.

BABY BEN'S BUSY BOOK, Ziefert, Harriet.
Baby Ben shows us the many things he can do. See also other Baby Ben books such as *BABY BEN GETS DRESSED.*

Books For Children Two to Five Years Old

MOONGAME, Asch, Frank.
Bear and his friend, Little Bird, play hide and seek with the moon in this favorite story of friendship and play. See also *MOONCAKE; HAPPY BIRTHDAY, MOON; BEAR SHADOW.*

ANIMALS SHOULD DEFINITELY NOT WEAR CLOTHING, Barrett, Judity.
Humorous idea expressed in brief text and comic drawings. See also *ANIMALS SHOULD DEFINITELY NOT ACT LIKE PEOPLE.*

BEAR FACTS, Bennett, David and Rosalinda Kightley, series.
These factual books look like picture books, but have a lot of information on subjects of interest to preschoolers. See also *DAY AND NIGHT; RAIN; EARTH; SEASONS.*

FLASH, CRASH, RUMBLE AND ROLL, Let's Read-And-Find-Out Science Book, Branley, Franklyn and Seymour Simon.
This is just one book in a series suitable for preschoolers. Books emphasize the natural world around us. See also *SNOW IS FALLING.*

MR. GUMPY'S OUTING, Burningham, John.
A cumulative story of what happens when Mr. Gumpy takes the animals for a ride in the country. It's sure to bring a smile of recognition to the face of the smallest listener.

Books For Children Two to Five Years Old (cont'd.)

FREIGHT TRAIN, Crews, Donald.
All children love trains and the graphic style of this picture book is perfect for this age group. Introduces the names of the various cars and begins to teach color recognition as well.

TOMIE DE PAOLA'S FAVORITE NURSERY TALES, DePaola, Tomie.
This collection of folk and fairy tales has been selected with younger children in mind. Contains many of the classic tales from Grimm, Andersen, and European folklore.

LITTLE RED HEN, Galdone, Paul.
This version of the famous story of the Little Red Hen who sows, reaps, and bakes without any help from her friends, is just right for the preschool set.

FILL IT UP — ALL ABOUT SERVICE STATIONS, Gibbons, Gail.
This author has written many books providing factual information on the simplest level on topics of interest to very young children. See also *FIRE! FIRE!; DEPARTMENT STORE; DINOSAURS; FLYING; SUN UP, SUN DOWN.*

BIG ONES, LITTLE ONE, Hoban, Tana.
Mother animals and their babies illustrate differences in size in this photographic picture book. Designed to teach concepts and visual discrimination. See also *ROUND & ROUND & ROUND; DOTS, SPOTS, SPECKLES AND STRIPES; CHILDREN'S ZOO; IS IT ROUGH? IS IT SMOOTH? IS IT SHINY?*

ROSIE'S WALK, Hutchins, Pat.
Rosie, the hen, miraculously escapes capture by a fox.

PAUL BUNYAN, Kellogg, Steven.
The story of Paul and his blue ox, Babe, is told in a style that is easily appreciated by preschoolers. See also *PECOS BILL; JOHNNY APPLESEED.*

THE THREE LITTLE PIGS, Marshall, James.
Tale in which one of three brother pigs survives a wolf's attacks by using his head and planning well. See also *RED RIDING HOOD; GOLDILOCKS AND THE THREE BEARS.*

PIG PIG GROWS UP, McPhail, David.
Pig Pig didn't want to grow up and his mother was sick and tired of it. Then, one day, Pig Pig saved the day and was never a baby again. See also *PIG PIG GOES TO CAMP; PIG PIG RIDES AGAIN; PIG PIG AND THE MAGIC PHOTO ALBUM.*

ROLL OVER, Peek, Merle.
Nicely illustrated version of the popular counting song. See also *MARY WORE HER RED DRESS; BALANCING ACT.*

Books For Children Two to Five Years Old (cont'd.)

CURIOUS GEORGE, Rey, H.A.
George, that curious little monkey, is always getting into trouble, but, with the help of his friend, the Man in the Yellow Hat, everything always works out just fine.

MY DOCTOR, Rockwell, Anne.
The picture book format of Anne Rockwell's books and cartoon characters illustrate topics of interest to youngsters. See also *MY DENTIST; FIRE ENGINES.*

MOVING (First Experience Books), Rogers, Fred.
Mr. Rogers has prepared a series of books dealing with the concerns and fears of toddlers and preschoolers. See also *GOING TO THE DOCTOR; GOING TO DAY CARE; MAKING FRIENDS; THE NEW BABY.*

THE RELATIVES CAME, Rylant, Cynthia.
The joy and warmth of loving families shines through in this book describing how it feels when the relatives come for their annual visit.

WHERE THE WILD THINGS ARE, Sendak, Maurice.
The classic picture book of our time, the night Max wore his wolf suit and made mischief of one kind and another, is something no child should miss.

THE MITTEN, Tresselt, Alvin.
A little boy loses his mitten and first a mouse, then a frog, an owl, a rabbit, a fox, a wolf, a boar, and a bear crawl in to get out of the cold weather. Find out what happens when the cricket tries to get into the mitten, too.

POLAR EXPRESS, VanAllsburg, Chris.
This story of a young boy's trip to the North Pole to receive the first gift of Christmas from Santa has already become a holiday favorite. See also *JUMANJI; THE WRECK OF THE ZEPHYR.*

AIR (Talkabout Series), Webb, Angela and Chris Fairclough.
This is one in a series of beautifully photographed books that provide information and simple experiments on a variety of topics. See also *SAND; WATER; SOIL.*

ELBERT'S BAD WORD, Wood, Audrey.
Elbert caught a bad word and shocked everyone at an elegant garden party. A helpful wizard teaches Elbert some acceptable alternatives and the bad word shrinks away.

HARRY THE DIRTY DOG, Zion, Gene (series).
The stories about Harry are just right for youngsters growing into stories. See also *HARRY BY THE SEA; NO ROSES FOR HARRY.*

Picture Books for School-Age Children

MISS NELSON IS MISSING, Allard

WHAT'S THE MATTER, SYLVIE, CAN'T YOU RIDE? Anderson

MOVE OVER, TWERP, Alexander

DAWN, Bang

GREY LADY AND THE STRAWBERRY SNATCHER, Bang

EVERYBODY NEEDS A ROCK, Baylor

GRANDFATHER TWILIGHT, Berger

PAIN AND THE GREAT ONE, Blume

GORILLA, Browne

MIKE MULLIGAN AND HIS STEAM SHOVEL, Burton

THE GHOST IN THE LAGOON, Carlson

THE TROUBLE WITH MOM, Cole

DINOSAURS AND BEASTS OF YORE, Cole

TOG THE RIBBER OR GRANNEY'S TALE, Coltman

MAGICIAN AND MCTEE, Coombs

TROUBLE FOR TRUMPETS, Cross

HELGA'S DOWRY: A TROLL LOVE STORY, DePaola

NOW ONE FOOT, NOW THE OTHER, DePaola

WHAT IS BEYOND THE HILL? Ekker

HOW DOES IT FEEL TO BE OLD? Farber

PATCHWORK QUILT, Flournoy

SOMEBODY STOLE SECOND, Foley

NORMAN THE DOORMAN, Freeman

HOW MY PARENTS LEARNED TO EAT, Friedman

ARNOLD OF THE DUCKS, Gerstein

SHE CAME BRINGING ME THAT LITTLE BABY GIRL, Greenfield

WITCH WHO LIVES DOWN THE HALL, Guthrie

OX-CART MAN, Hall

ESTEBAN AND THE GHOST, Hancock

AMANDA AND THE WITCH SWITCH, Himmelman

ADVENTURES OF CHARLIE AND HIS WHEAT STRAW HAT, Hiser

BEN'S TRUMPET, Isadora

MAX, Isadora

WHEN PANDA CAME TO OUR HOUSE, Jensen

ROUND TRIP, Jones

CHICKEN LITTLE, Kellogg

FIRST TULIPS IN HOLLAND, Krasilovsky

GONDOLIER OF VENICE, Krauss

PHILHARMONIC GETS DRESSED, Kuskin

MERRY EVER AFTER, Lasker

ALEXANDER AND THE WIND-UP MOUSE, Lionni

WHERE THE RIVER BEGINS, Locker

BOO TO A GOOSE, Low

FLOSSIE AND THE FOX, McKissack

CUT-UPS, Marshall

GEORGE AND MARTHA TONS OF FUN, Marshall

FOOLISH RABBIT'S BIG MISTAKE, Martin

MRS. BEGGS AND THE WIZARD, Mayer

UNICORN AND THE LAKE, Mayer

WHINNIE THE LOVESICK DRAGON, Mayer

GREEDY ZEBRA, Mwenye

SAM, BANGS AND MOONSHINE, Ness

Picture Books for School-Age Children (cont'd.)

THE DAY JIMMY'S BOA ATE THE WASH, Noble

CHURCH MOUSE, Oakley

MIRRORSTONE, Palin

ZELLA, ZACK AND ZODIAC, Peet

GRANDPA BEAR, Pryor

STAGE DOOR TO TERROR, Quackenbush

GARTH PIG AND THE ICE CREAM LADY, Rayner

WAITING FOR SPRING STORIES, Roberts

SOUP FOR SUPPER, Root

I'M COMING TO GET YOU, Ross

RELATIVE CAME, Rylant

WHEN I WAS YOUNG IN THE MOUNTAINS, Rylant

MATT'S MITT, Sachs

ALISTAIR'S TIME MACHINE, Sadler

LEGEND OF SLEEPY HOLLOW, San Souci

HOW MUCH IS A MILLION? Schwartz

BUTTER BATTLE BOOK, Seuss

GILA MONSTERS MEET YOU AT THE AIRPORT, Sharmat

BIG FAT ENORMOUS LIE, Sharmat

FROG BAND AND THE ONION SELLER, Smith

MRS. MINETTA'S CAR POOL, Spurr

GOOD LUCK PENCIL, Stanley

AMOS AND BORIS, Steig

DOCTOR DESOTO, Steig

STEVIE, Steptoe

NO FRIENDS, Stevenson

PLANET OF LOST THINGS, Strand

GARDEN OF ABDUL GASAZI, Van Allsburg

JUMANJI, Van Allsburg

MYSTERIES OF HARRIS BURDICK, Van Allsburg

ALEXANDER AND THE TERRIBLE HORRIBLE, NO GOOD, VERY BAD DAY, Viorst

IRA SLEEPS OVER, Waber

BROTHER TO THE WIND, Walter

TY'S ONE-MAN BAND, Walter

TIMOTHY GOES TO SCHOOL, Wells

BETWEEN CATTAILS, Williams

CHAIR FOR MY MOTHER, Williams

DUFFY AND THE DEVIL, Zemach

I Can Read

first grade

1st Grade — 1st Semester

AND I MEAN IT, STANLEY   Bonsall, C.
A super creation is destroyed when Stanley, the
dog, rushes to greet his little boy.

DAY I HAD TO PLAY WITH MY SISTER   Bonsall, C.
A boy tries to play hide 'n' seek with his baby
sister who is much too young for the game.

MINE'S THE BEST   Bonsall, C.
Each of two boys is convinced that his water
float is the very best.

WHO'S AFRAID OF THE DARK   Bonsall, C.
A boy has a dog that is afraid of the dark.

WITCH WHO FORGOT   Carley, W.
A witch has trouble getting ready for a party
because she is so forgetful.

WHO WILL BE MY FRIEND?   Hoff, S.
When Freddy moves to a new home he must
make all new friends.

MY HANDS CAN   Holzenthaler, J.
How many things can you do with your hands?

FOLLOW THE MONSTERS   Lerner, S.
Sesame Street monsters are on their way home.

WHAT HAVE I GOT   McClintock, M.
Wonderful things happen to a boy who has a
pocketful of odds and ends.

CAT AT BAT   Stadler, J.
Phonetic rhyming lines featuring an assortment of
animals such as "A snail is on a tail with the mail."

HENRY'S BUSY DAY   Campbell, R.
Henry, the puppy, keeps going all day long
doing all the many things he likes.

CAROUSEL   Crews, D.
Take a wild ride on a merry-go-round.

JAMBERRY   Degen, B.
A bear and a boy have an adventure finding
berries for jam.

CLAUDE THE DOG   Gackenbach, D.
Claude gives away everything he owns on
Christmas Day.

CHICK AND THE DUCKLING   Ginsburg, M.
A chick thinks he's a duckling.

GOOD MORNING, CHICK   Ginsburg, M.
Chick hatches from an egg one morning and
finds out that life is an adventure.

FOLLOW THE LEADER   Hann, J.
A group of children play follow-the-leader up the
hill, over the wall, and into an adventure.

PAT THE CAT   Hawkins, C.
See also
JEN THE HEN
MIG THE PIG
All beginning readers will enjoy an orange cat
and some marvelous adventures. This is
especially appropriate for children who are
learning to read phonetically.

SPOT'S FIRST WALK   Hill, E.
Spot, a puppy, goes exploring on his own.

WHERE'S SPOT   Hill, E.
Spot's mom goes looking for him so he can eat
his supper.

WAKE UP, JEREMIAH   Himler, R.
Jeremiah wakes early and greets the sun in his
special way.

ONE LITTLE KITTEN   Hoban, T.
Read about all the antics of a small kitten.

DON'T FORGET THE BACON   Hutchins, P.
A boy, sent to the store with a long list of
purchases, promptly mixes them up.

WHOSE MOUSE ARE YOU   Kraus, R.
A young mouse reunites his family in this fantasy.

SAM'S CAR   Lindgren, B.
After trading blows, Sam and Lisa find a happier
solution to their problem.

KITTEN CAN   McMillan, B.
Kittens can do many things, from climbing
to eating.

I CAN RIDE IT   Watanabe, S.
A little bear shows all the ways he can ride,
including an unusual way to use roller skates.

COUNT THE CATS   Weins, Erika
One to ten cats can have lots of fun.

MARMALADE'S NAP   Wheeler, C.
Marmalade, the cat, has to look hard to find a
quiet place to sleep.

MARMALADE'S SNOWY DAY   Wheeler, C.
Marmalade, the cat, goes out on a winter day to
play in the snow.

CAKE STORY   Wolcott, P.
When bear bakes a cake, all the animals come
to eat it.

1st Grade — 2nd Semester

LEO AND EMILY   Brandenberg, L.
Emily and Leo learn to get dressed in the dark,
swap a wig and a rabbit, and put on a
magic show.

EMPTY SQUIRREL   Carrick, C.
Three stories about a boy named Paul who is
good at taking care of pets, and even knows
what to do with an "empty squirrel."

WHO'S AFRAID OF THE DARK?   Bonsall, C.
Stella, the dog, is afraid of the dark.

WILLY BEAR   Kantrowitz, M.
Willy Bear has a hard time sleeping the night
before his first day of school.

POISON IVY CASE   Lexau, J.
When Willy is falsely accused of not keeping his
sister in their yard, he enlists the aid of a novice
witch to prove his innocence.

DAY WITH FROG AND TOAD   Lobell, A.
Frog and Toad are good friends and have many
adventures and fun times together.

BIG BEAR, SPARE THAT TREE   Margolis, R.
Big Bear comes to the rescue of Mrs. Jay and her
babies.

THREE BY THE SEA   Marshall, E.
Holly, Spider and Sam try to see who can tell
the scariest story when they are relaxing at
the seashore.

JED'S JUNIOR SPACE PATROL   Marzollo, J.
This is a wonderful story with a teddy bear robot
and two creatures called cogs.

KISS FOR LITTLE BEAR   Minarik, E.
Little Bear draws a picture for his grandmother
which she loves.

TEACH US, AMELIA BEDELIA   Parish, P.
Follow the hilarious antics of Amelia Bedelia.

MONDAY I WAS AN ALLIGATOR   Pearson, S.
Emily has her family in an uproar when she
imagines herself to be many strange animals.

PAPA'S LEMONADE AND OTHER STORIES Rice, E.
Mama and Papa believe in making the best of
everything, even making lemonade without
lemons.

GREG'S MICROSCOPE   Selsam, M.
Greg gets a microscope and his whole family
becomes interested in using it to observe
common household items.

STORY OF BENTLEY   Sharmat, M.
Bentley finds that sometimes life is sad and often
scary, but mostly very good.

TALES OF OLIVER PIG AND MORE
                              VanLeewen, J.
Meet the Pig family, and follow their everyday
adventures from making mud pies with raisins to
a walk in the snow.

ABU ALI: TALES OF THE MIDDLE EAST
                              VanWoerkom, D.
Three folktales about Abu Ali, who fools his friends
and even fools himself.

WE ARE BEST FRIENDS   Aliki
Robert is lost without his best friend, Peter, until he
finds a new friend, Will.

HAPPY BIRTHDAY, MOON   Asch, F.
Bear finds out its the moon's birthday and
decides to give him a present.

DARK, DARK TALE   Brown, R.
Travel to a dark, dark house up dark, dark stairs
to a dark, dark corner and a dark, dark box.

TROUBLE WITH MOM   Cole, B.
Having a mother who is a witch causes problems
for the new boy at school until disaster strikes.

DAY IS WAITING   Freeman, D.
There are wonderful things to see and do each
and every day.

THREE KITTENS   Ginsburg, M.
Three kittens, black, white and gray, change
colors as they play.

WILBERFORCE GOES ON A PICNIC   Gordon, M.
Follow Wilberforce from sunup to sundown on a
very special day — the day of the picnic.

UP DAY DOWN DAY   Hann, J.
On a fishing trip, one friend catches a fish and
another a cold.

ALFIE'S FEET   Hughes, S.
Alfie gets a new pair of shoes, but something is
just not right.

ALFIE GETS IN FIRST   Hughes, S.
Alfie accidentally locks his mother out of the
house and he can't reach the door knob.

TEN SLEEPY SHEEP   Keller, H.
Louis can't sleep, so he counts sheep. Each
sheep brings a surprise for the sleepless party.

FIX-IT   McPhail, D.
A broken television leads Emma to more exciting
activities.

WHO TOOK THE FARMER'S HAT   Nodset, J.
The farmer's favorite old brown hat has found a
new use.

CLEMENS' KINGDOM   Demarest, C.
Clemens, a lion statue, explores the treasure
within his library kingdom.

THE SURPRISE   Shannon, G.
Squirrel comes up with a good idea for his
mother's birthday.

RED IS BEST   Stinson, K.
Kelly loves the color red. She loves her red coat,
red stockings, red cup, and red paint, because
red makes her feel so good.

SOPHIE AND JACK   Taylor, J.
Can you help Sophie find Jack when they play
hide and seek?

SOPHIE AND JACK HELP OUT   Taylor, J.
Two young hippos, Sophie and Jack, help out in
the spring garden, causing some surprises at
harvest time.

IF YOU TAKE A PENCIL   Testa, F.
Pencil drawings come to life as you count
through the pages to find a treasure.

BRAVO, ERNEST AND CELESTINE   Vincent, G.
Ernest and Celestine earn money as street
performers.

ERNEST AND CELESTINE   Vincent, G.
Ernest cheers Celestine up when she loses her
favorite doll.

ERNEST AND CELESTINE'S PICNIC   Vincent, G.
Ernest and Celestine have a rainy day picnic.

MARMALADE'S PICNIC   Wheeler, C.
A surprise in the picnic basket will delight
beginning readers.

PRINCESS AND FROGGIE   Zemach, H.
Whenever the Princess has a problem she can't
solve, Froggie helps out.

I Can Write

second grade

2nd Grade — 1st Semester

TURKEY GIRL   Baker, Betty
Tally has no family except for the mayor's turkeys, until her bravery helps her find a new home.

A DOG I KNOW   Brenner, Barbara
Getting to know all the fun things about a special dog.

IG LIVES IN A CAVE   Champman, Carol
Have you ever wondered what it would be like to live in a cave? Join Ig on his many adventures as a cave dweller.

LONGEST FLOAT IN THE PARADE   Carrick, Carol
Jimmy and Pinky, disgusted with Darleen's idea of a float, make their own — the longest one of all.

ALEX AND THE CAT   Griffith, Helen
Alex, dissatisfied with his lot, wants to change. The cat quietly shows him that everything and everyone has some advantages.

MORE ALEX AND THE CAT   Griffith, Helen
Three more stories about Alex and his friend the cat, which include the long buried bone, mitten chewing, and a snowflake chase in the winter.

CROW AND MRS. GADDY   Gage, Wilson
What does Mrs. Gaddy do with a tricky, mean, old crow who drops a bug into her milk and breaks her glasses?

LAZIEST ROBOT IN ZONE ONE
                    Hoban, Lillian and Phoebe
Danger lurks when Sol-1 and his robot friends form a search party to find Big Red Rover before their Down Time.

SURPRISES   Hopkins, Lee Bennett
If you ever wonder about marshmallow puff boats whiffing down the river, if you sometimes hum yourself to sleep, and have a special place for keepsakes, then leap through the surprise verses.

OLD TURTLE'S WINTER GAMES   Kessler, Leonard
Old Turtle tries to have fun in the cold and snow by creating winter game contests for his animal pals.

THE STRAW MAID   Lobel, Anita
Ingenuity enables a girl to trick the three robbers who forced her to cook and clean for them.

ROBIN OF BRAY   Marzollo, Jean and Claudio
With the aid of a magic wand, Robin is able to rescue the Princess of Bray.

AMY GOES FISHING   Marzollo, Jean
Amy has an adventure when she goes fishing with her father.

HARRY'S VISIT   Porte, Barbara
Harry just knew that he would hate visiting boring Aunt Betty and Uncle Charlie. But was he in for a big surprise.

WHAT I DID LAST SUMMER   Prelutsky, Jack
Poems about a boy's fun-filled summer vacation from the euphoric last day of school to the boring days of August.

FUNNY BUNNIES   Quackenbush, Robert
Too many bunnies crowd into one small hotel room.

HENRY'S AWFUL MISTAKE   Quackenbush, Robert
Before his guest Clara comes to dinner, Henry, the duck, tries to get rid of a little ant.

UP A TALL TREE   Rockwell, Ann
Nick finds adventure and magic in the woods and grows up to be a very wise man with a special secret.

M & M AND THE BIG BAG   Ross, Pat
Mandi and Mimi are off again — this time for a trip to the Big Bag Supermarket with a list that sort of gets chewed.

HOME ALONE   Schick, Eleanor
Andy's first afternoon home alone after school, when Mom starts her new job, shows his ability to cope with apprehension, loneliness, and responsibility.

JOEY ON HIS OWN   Schick, Eleanor
Joey is sent to the store all alone for the first time, and real and imagined fears disappear as he happily buys the bread for lunch.

THERE IS A CARROT IN MY EAR & OTHER NOODLE TALES   Schwartz, A.
The Brosn family, have amusing and unusual adventures because they are noodle-heads.

IT'S ME, HIPPO   Thaler, Mike
Hippo learns that everyone is different but they still can be friends.

MOONCAKE   Asch, Frank
Bear would like to taste the moon, so he builds a rocketship to get there.

YOU MAKE THE ANGELS CRY   Cazet, Denys
When Albert gets a cookie for a snack, the wind knocks over the cookie jar, breaking it, and Albert's mother becomes angry with him.

BONY-LEGS   Cole, Joanna
Sasha's only hope of escape from Bony-Legs lies in a goat, a dog, and a cat.

LITTLE WITCH AND THE RIDDLE   Degen, Bruce
Little Witch and her friend Otto adventure
together, seeking the answer to a riddle.

LEO, ZACK AND EMMIE   Ehrlich, Amy
Leo, Zack, and the new girl in town, Emmie,
share Halloween adventures, show-and-tell, and
finally, friendship.

POSY   Pomerantz, Charlotte
Posy loves to hear stories of when she was little,
such as the time when she ordered pink sheets.

BIG FAT ENORMOUS LIE   Sharmat, Marjorie
A child's small lie becomes a big, fat, enormous
monster.

PEABODY   Wells, Rosemary
Peabody is a teddy bear, temporarily relegated
to the back corner when Annie receives Rita, a
talking doll, for her birthday.

2nd Grade — 2nd Semester

MY DOG AND THE KEY MYSTERY   Adler, David
Jennie's dog, who likes to solve mysteries, saves
the day by finding her friend's missing key.

THE NEW HOUSE   Cauley, Lorinda Bryan
The woodchuck family wants to buy a new
home, but when they try to sell their old home,
they decide it is the best one after all.

SLUG WHO THOUGHT HE WAS A SNAIL
          Cauley, Lorinda Bryan
Sam, the slug, is in search of a new place to live.
Then his friends decide that he is not a slug, but a
snail without a shell.

PICTURE PIE   Emberley, Ed
A circle-drawing book that shows how to cut a
basic circle into flowers, birds of many feathers,
clowns, fish, borders and more.

BLACK BEAR BABY   Freschet, Bereniece
Mischief and adventure come to two bear cubs
in their life in the wild.

MAN WHO ENTERED A CONTEST
          Krasilovsky, Phyllis
A man who loved to bake cakes entered a
cake-baking contest and won with a little
accidental help from his cat.

CATS ARE GOOD COMPANY   Landshoff, Ursula
See also
OKAY, GOOD DOG
Learn about cats and their behavior.

MISS HAPP IN THE POISON IVY CASE   Lexau, J.
How did Tilly get poison ivy when Willy didn't let
her out of the yard?

HOCUS AND POCUS AT THE CIRCUS
          Manushkin, Fran
Hocus tries to teach little sister Pocus to be as
mean a little witch as her older sister.

RED SUN GIRL   Marzollo, Jean and Claudio
Kiri is a girl who is unhappy because she doesn't
change into an animal like other family
members.

RUTHIE'S RUDE FRIENDS   Marzollo, Jean
Ruthie is the only kid from Earth on Planet X10,
where she is teased because she doesn't have
fish scales or pig ears, and she can't fly.

LITTLE WILD ELEPHANT   Michel, Anna
Learn about the growth and development of a
wild baby African elephant.

LITTLE WILD LION CUB   Michel, Anna
Little Lion learns many things as he grows up by
watching the big lions in his family.

CORNSTALKS AND CANNONBALLS

Mitchell, Barbara

Cornstalks, rakes, and hoes helped the brave citizens of Lewes, Delaware, win a battle with the English in 1812.

HORTENSE

Paul, J. S.

A silly repetitive tale of Hortense Hen's search for her new baby chick.

I WAS A SECOND GRADE WEREWOLF

Pinkwater, Daniel

Lawrence Talbot spends 24 hours as a werewolf, but no one notices.

ANTS

Pluckrose, Henry

Did you know that ants are very much like humans? They eat, work, protect each other, and even kiss.

BIG KITE CONTEST

Ruthstrom, Dorotha

Stephen's bat-wing kite gets torn and he tries to earn money for a new one in time for the kite contest; but it is his sister's idea that is the winner.

SEA OTTERS

Shaw, Evelyn

A science book telling about sea otters and their lives will delight readers.

HONEST ANDREW

Skurzynski, Gloria

An otter ought to be honest, but Andrew finds he has to be nice as well.

HEDGEHOG SURPRISES

Stanovish, Betty Jo

Woodchuck has a difficult time convincing Hedgehog that the world won't fall apart before he can show his surprise at Black Bear's birthday party.

COMMANDER TOAD AND THE BIG BLACK HOLE

Yolen, Jane

Can Commander Toad and his fearless crew keep their space ship Star Warts out of danger as they approach the Black Hole?

COMMANDER TOAD IN SPACE

Yolen, Jane

Commander Toad and his companions land on a mysterious planet.

AUNT NINA AND HER NEPHEWS AND NIECES

Brandenberg, Franz

Aunt Nina's nieces and nephews have a wonderful time at her cat Fluffy's birthday party. But the guest of honor is missing.

ALFIE GIVES A HAND

Hughes, Shirley

Alfie is invited to Bernard's birthday party and takes his security blanket along, but finds he no longer needs it.

ROUND TRIP

Jonas, Ann

Start out on a trip to the city in the morning and turn the book around for the trip at night.

A WOLF STORY

McPhail, David

A wolf, captured to be in the movies, is saved by some school children who understand that wolves need to be free.

WHEN I WAS YOUNG IN THE MOUNTAINS

Rylant, Cynthia

A little girl remembers what it was like growing up in the mountains with her grandparents.

MY TEACHER SLEEPS IN SCHOOL

Weiss, Leatie

Mrs. Marsh's class gets a surprise when they think she sleeps in school.

FIRE FIGHTERS

Broekel, Ray

This colorful book tells all about fire fighters, their equipment, clothes, and even how to become a fire fighter.

BIRDS WE KNOW

Friskey, Margaret

Colored photographs help tell us about many kinds of birds, including fascinating facts about their bodies, nests and life-styles.

WHALES AND OTHER SEA MAMMALS

Posell, Elsa

Children will enjoy this book as it tells the exciting story of whales and whaling in words and colored pictures.

I Can Discover

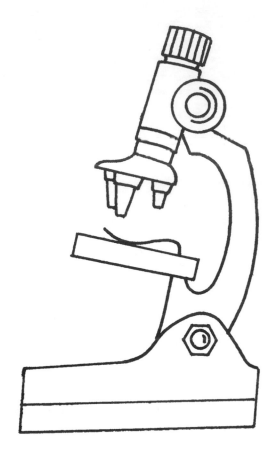

third grade

ROBOT BIRTHDAY   Bunting, Eve
Everything is A-OK when Mom's present of a special birthday robot makes adjusting to their new neighborhood easier for the twins.

DOGGONE MYSTERY   Christian, Mary
What clever mastermind is robbing the neighbors? Clara, Jason, and their dog, Ruffles, go all-out to solve the mystery and close the case.

BRIMHALL TURNS DETECTIVE   Dalton, Judy
Playing detective proves to be a funny adventure for Brimhall, the bear.

LITTLE WILD LION CUB   Michel, Anna
Learning to roar and hunt are all part of growing up in a family of wild lion cubs.

THAT DOG   Newman, Nanette
After the death of his favorite dog, Ben is sure he'll never want another dog. Ben changes his mind when a stray dog follows him home.

WHAT I DID LAST SUMMER   Prelutsky, Jack
Summer fun starts out with sand in the nose and progresses through a burning throat, a crushed guitar and a camp full of ants. Maybe school is better.

BUSY BUZZING BUMBLEBEES & OTHER TONGUE TWISTERS   Schwartz, Alvin
Twist your mouth around lots of tongue twisters like, "Big Bill blew big blue bubbles." Difficult to say, but easy to read.

FIRST AMERICANS: TRIBES OF NORTH AMERICA
                              Watson, Jane
The Indians were the first Americans — read
about their homes, their work, and the games
they played.

MICE ON ICE   Yolen, Jane
Gomer, the rat king, mousenaps Rosa, the star of
Mouse Ice Capades, and demands the secret
ice formula for the ransom.

SLEEPING UGLY   Yolen, Jane
Princess Miserella, although beautiful, was the
meanest, wickedest, and most worthless princess
around. Her bad temper and even worse
manners anger a fairy into casting a spell that
puts everyone to sleep for hundreds of years.

ONE IN THE MIDDLE IS THE GREEN KANGAROO
                              Blume, Judy
Being the middle kid in a family can be hard for
Freddy, but exciting things happen when he
becomes the only green kangaroo in the school
play.

CLANCY'S COAT   Bunting, Eve
Tippett, the tailor, had difficulty in returning
Farmer Clancy's old coat, but he is quick to find
a solution to mend a broken friendship.

GHOST IN THE LAGOON   Carlson, Natalie
On Halloween, Timmy decides to confront the
ghost that has been scaring his family when they
try to catch catfish for dinner.

MAGICIAN & MCTREE   Coombs, Patricia
When the magician's cat, McTree, falls into a
magic potion, he comes out talking.

FAIR'S FAIR   Garfield, Leon
Jackson, a bedraggled street orphan, is led to a
strange mansion by a large black dog.

ARNOLD OF THE DUCKS   Gerstein, Mordicai
When Arnold is taken from his wading pool by a
nearsighted pelican and dropped into a nest of
wood ducks, he becomes such a good duck
that it is hard to go back to being a boy.

PROBLEM WITH PULCIFER   Heide, Florence
Pulcifer's parents worry a lot, because he'd
rather read than watch television.

MIDNIGHT CASTLE   Joerns, Consuelo
A family of mice discover tin people living in a
castle who come to life at the stroke of midnight.

FIRST TULIPS IN HOLLAND   Krasilovsky, Phyllis
A special love story of how the tulips were
introduced to Holland.

WILD BABY GOES TO SEA   Lindgren, Barbro
Ben's surprising escapades multiply as he sails the
seas unafraid and full of the spirit of adventure.

THROUGH GRANDPA'S EYES
                          MacLachlan, Patricia
John learns a different way of seeing the world
through his blind grandfather.

SPACE CASE   Marshall, Edward
Halloween may be the worst time for a Martian
to visit earth — or the best.

VEGETABLE THIEVES   Moore, Inga
There are vegetable thieves aboard! Des and
Letty Mouse are so tired from gardening that
they don't see or hear the culprits.

BLACK PEARL & THE GHOST   Myers, Walter
Dr. Aramy, with the help of Dr. Dribble, the ghost
catcher, finds the stolen pearl and catches the
thief in this funny mystery.

IN MY TREEHOUSE   Schertie, Alice
A whole new world is discovered from the view
of a treehouse.

FRIZZY THE FEARFUL   Sharmat, Marjorie
Frizzy is scared of everything until Nova Cat
teaches him how to be brave.

JAMANJI   VanAllsburg, Chris
Play adventures on a jungle board game is one
thing, but what happens when the game
becomes real?

STORIES ABOUT ROSIE   Voight, Cynthia
Rosie is a dog who believes her family's job is
solely to take care of her every whim and need.

*CAM JANSEN & THE MYSTERY OF THE BABE RUTH
BASEBALL*   Adler, David
Cam Jansen uses her amazing photographic
memory to find the person who stole a valuable
autographed baseball.

*CAM JANSEN & THE MYSTERY OF THE GOLDEN
COINS*   Adler, David
When her science fair project disappears, Cam
Jansen uses her amazing photographic memory
to solve the mystery and in the process discovers
two very valuable coins.

LIONEL & THE SPY NEXT DOOR   Allen, Linda
Lionel's attempts to spy on the new neighbor
create havoc in the neighborhood.

WARREN WEASEL'S WORSE THAN MEASLES
          Bach, Alice
Warren Weasel thinks he is a loser until his friend,
Bear, shows him a few winning tricks.

KATY DID IT   Boutis, Victoria
Backpacking with Dad is a special treat for Katy
until she finds out that the trail is steep, the food is
awful, and there may be bears.

CLUCK ONE   Mathews, Louise
Weasel attempts to fool Mr. Cluck by slipping an
assortment of eggs into Mrs. Cluck's nest.

NIGHT THE MONSTER CAME   Calhoun, Mary
Giant footprints in the snow, strange noises in the
night, and the sight of a big, furry figure in the
distance make nine-year-old Andy fearful that
Bigfoot is lurking in the Great North Woods.

*STORIES JULIAN TELLS PLUS MORE STORIES JULIAN
TELLS*   Cameron, Ann
Julian tells little brother, Huey, exciting stories by
using his big imagination and his talent for
getting into trouble.

*SEBASTIAN (SUPER SLEUTH) AND THE BONE TO PICK
MYSTERY*   Christian, Mary
Sebastian, the dog detective, uncovers a fraud
involving dinosaur bones while investigating a
case of breaking and entering at the local
museum.

RAMONA QUIMBY — AGE 8   Cleary, Beverly
Third grade is a tough year for Ramona. The
school bully is after her, she gets raw eggs in her
hair, and she even throws up in school.

300-POUND CAT   Dauer, Rosamond
William Cat's taste for unusual foods — turnips,
typewriters, and boots — leads to several
hilarious situations.

WARTON AND THE CASTAWAYS   Erickson, Russell
Being trapped on a floating tree with a hungry
raccoon during a flood is no fun for the two Toad
Brothers.

STONE FOX   Gardiner, John
Little Willy needs to win the dog sled race in order
to save grandfather's farm.

FISH FACE   Giff, Patricia
Poor Emily is in a dilemma! No one believes her
when she discovers that the newcomer in the
class is a thief.

MOUSEWIFE   Godden, Rumer
Mousewife is frightened by the fluttering of wings
as she creeps into a cage searching for food.

BOY WHO WANTED A FAMILY   Gordon, Shirley
Michael experiences the hopes and fears of
having a new adoptive mother.

THADDEUS   Herzig, Alison & Mali, Jane
How lucky can you be? Thaddeus has an
uncle who writes a book just about him — and
it's all true!

CHIPS AND JESSIE   Hughes, Shirley
Chips and his friend, Jessie, have many
adventures, from losing the class hamster to
selling a customer's stole at a rummage sale.

ADVENTURES OF ALI BABA BERNSTEIN
                                Hurwitz, Johanna
There were just too many David Bernsteins — four
in his class and seventeen in the phone book —
so David becomes Ali Baba.

ME & MY SISTER CLARA   Inkiow, Dimiter
Clara and her brother go through many fun
adventures with their parents and relatives.

ADAM DRAWS HIMSELF A DRAGON
                                Korschunow, Irina
Adam befriends a small dragon who has left
dragon land because he doesn't fit in.

LOST AND FOUND   Little, Jean
Lucy finds a lost dog and rapidly becomes
attached to it, but has to face the prospect of
giving it back to its real owner.

SEVEN KISSES IN A ROW   MacLachlan, Patricia
Everyone is different! That is Emma's discovery
when her aunt and uncle come to stay while her
parents attend a convention.

DON'T BE MAD, IVY   McDonnell, Christine
Ivy is always ready to try something new in these
six adventures.

BE A PERFECT PERSON IN JUST THREE DAYS
                                Manes, Stephen
Milo can be perfect if, among other things, he's
willing to wear a stalk of broccoli around his neck
for 24 hours.

CHRISTMAS PRESENT MYSTERY
                                Markham, Marion
Katy and Mickey are determined to find out how
the mysterious face appeared in the Christmas
family photo.

HALLOWEEN CANDY MYSTERY
                                Markham, Marion
Kate and Mickey find a diamond ring in their
trick-or-treat bag.

*CHAMELEON THE SPY & THE TERRIBLE TOASTER
TRAP*   Massie, Diane
Chameleon, the famous color-changing spy,
needs to work fast to find out who is putting
everyone in Beantown to sleep and then
robbing them.

HOW I FOUND MYSELF AT THE FAIR   Mauser, Par
Lost and alone in the crowded fairground, Laura
wonders how she will ever find her family.

MY WAR WITH MRS. GALLOWAY   Orgel, Doris
Rebecca wages war on Mrs. Galloway, the strict
babysitter who watches her while her
doctor/mother is working.

WAITING FOR SPRING   Roberts, Bethany
In order to pass time during the long winter
months, Father Rabbit tells stories to his family.

NIGHTMARE ISLAND   Roy, Ron
Scoop's first overnight camping trip becomes a
nightmare when he and older brother, Harley,
become trapped on Little Island by an oil
spill fire.

FLUNKING OF JOSHUA T. BATES   Shreve, Susan
Joshua has to repeat third grade. Taking his hurt
out on other kids doesn't help, but an understanding teacher does.

COMEBACK DOG   Thomas, Jane
Daniel hopes the half-starved, nearly frozen dog
he has nursed back to health will love him the
way Captain did, but when Lady has recovered,
she only snarls at Daniel and then she runs away.

BENJY & THE POWER OF ZINGIES
                                VanLeeuwen, Jean
Benjy needs (or thinks he does) real muscle to
get even with Alex. Is Zingies cereal really the
answer?

GIANT'S APPRENTICE   Wetterer, Margaret
Lian, the blacksmith's apprentice, is captured by
a giant. The blacksmith uses his wits and strength
to save the boy.

MITZE & THE ELEPHANTS   Williams, Barbara
Mitze's friendship with Ed, a zookeeper, leads to
her saving the life of a sick elephant.

THREE DAYS ON A RIVER IN A RED CANOE
Williams, Vera
Share in this exciting adventure of taking a shower under a waterfall, using scouring powder, and much more.

DINOSAURS BEWARE! Brown, Marc
Accident prevention is a lot more fun when dinosaurs rule the land and provide the safety tips.

DOCTOR CHANGE Cole, Joanne
Tom must read Doctor Change's spell books in order to escape from his slave-like existence.

SNOW QUEEN Andersen, Hans
Gerda must search all over the world for her friend, Kai, after he is kidnapped by the Snow Queen.

SUN UP, SUN DOWN Gibbons, Gail
Gaily colored illustrations make learning new things about the sun exciting.

HIAWATHA Longfellow, Henry
Longfellow's classic poem of an Indian boy's closeness to his natural surroundings is presented with new illustrations.

ANIMALS OF SEA AND SHORE Podendorf, Illa
Things to know and new words to learn enhance the exploration of information about the animals that live in or near the sea.

WHIFF, SNIFF, NIBBLE, AND CHEW
Pomerantz, Charlotte
The gingerbread boy escapes from the wicked old man who wants to eat him, only to find other dangers awaiting him.

FIRST LOOK AT BIRDS
Selsam, Millicent & Hunt, Joyce
This is a book of observations, not only interesting facts about birds, but also visual puzzles for the reader to study.

BEAVER Sheehan, Angela
Day-to-day life for the beaver is not so carefree. He must confront lynx, bear, and wolf while he raises his family.

YOU CAN'T MAKE A MOVE WITHOUT YOUR MUSCLES Showers, Paul
The human body has over 600 muscles. Any movement would be impossible without muscles.

TIMES (A NEW TRUE BOOK) Ziner, Feenie
Time and its measurement are always fascinating. In this book, all kinds of clocks are shown and their mechanics explained.

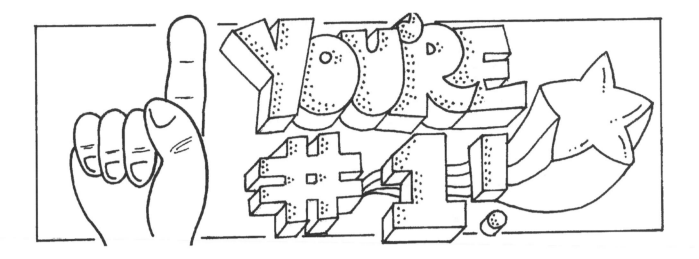

Rewards & Incentives

Children always enjoy a special acknowledgment for something well done. Often, just noticing their extra effort or their good attitude goes a long way in encouraging a positive attitude toward learning. Following are some ideas to show your appreciation for their work or behavior.

The reward coupons can be personalized and used for schoolwork as well as any other behavior or attitude that warrants reinforcement.

The educational rewards are a great way to show that their work was noticed.

Pencil toppers and bookmarks are another fun way to acknowledge a job well done.

Also included are a multiplication matrix and a pattern for flash cards, both invaluable tools in a child's education.

Reward Coupons

A coupon is a great way to show a child how proud you are of him or her. Several examples of reward coupons follow. Cut them out and allow the child to color them. Then, whenever a child finishes reading a book on his or her list, offer a coupon that can be spent for a night out with Dad, staying up an extra half hour, a movie rental of the child's choice, an ice cream cone, or a picnic at the park.

Educational Rewards

Copy several of these cards, color them and keep them handy. Whenever a child does an extra special job reading, writing, or spelling, slip a card into his book, onto her pillow, or into his backpack.

Pencil Toppers

A creative incentive for children is a pencil topper. On the following pages you will find samples of some ideas you can use to create pencil toppers. Reproduce onto white or colored paper, color, cut out, snip paper at the Xs and slide pencil through. A great idea for classroom awards or birthday treats.

207

Book Marks

Children seem to love bookmarks. They can never have too many. They are especially meaningful when they are personalized. A few ideas for bookmarks can be found below. Use these or create your own. Copy onto cardstock, cut out, color, and laminate for more durability. A new one can be given for each new book.

Multiplication Matrix

To help your children learn their multiplication tables, a matrix is provided below. Copy it and have your child fill it out, laminate if desired, and you have an excellent educational tool. When presented this way, a child often is able to see patterns not grasped when presented in other ways.

X	0	1	2	3	4	5	6	7	8	9	10	11	12
0													
1													
2													
3													
4													
5													
6													
7													
8													
9													
10													
11													
12													

Flash Cards

Surviving Your Trip

Kids oN the-Go

Table of Contents

Kids on the Go

Introduction

Vacation planning usually starts out full of excitement and anticipation. But often the reality of traveling with young children leaves us exhausted and discouraged.

Nothing works perfectly all the time, but hopefully there are some ideas in this chapter that will help you survive that trip.

There are simple games to play, tips on organizing, and ideas to encourage children to get along together.

Above all, try to relax and enjoy the journey as well as the destination.

Kids on the Go

It's time for our trip
I'm so excited
We've waited so long
And the kids are delighted.

It's been a long year
While we've planned and prepared
We saved lots of money
And the car is repaired.

I grabbed the dry cleaning
And mended my pants
I cancelled the paper
And watered the plants.

I washed all the clothes
They are packed nice and tight.
The dog is in the kennel —
He should be all right.

The car is all clean
The mail has been stopped
Lessons were cancelled
And the floor has been mopped.

I've changed my appointments.
The lawn is now mowed.
Believe it or not
The car is ready to load!

I know this sounds
Like a sticky situation,
But I think I'm too tired
To go on vacation!

Safety Rules for Traveling in the Car

Buckle Up

Children should always be buckled up or in a child safety seat. It is often difficult on long trips to enforce this rule. Try stopping for short stops to get out and stretch. Walk around the car or do a few jumping jacks, then change seating arrangements.

Don't Touch

Children need to know that there are important parts of a car that they should not touch while driving — door handles, gear shifts, ignition key, or door locks.

Keep All of You Inside

Hands, arms, and heads should never be hung out the window.

Keep the Noise Down

Loud music and upsetting noise can be frustrating and distracting to the driver.

5. Don't Block Driver's View

Don't pack the car so full that the driver can't see out the windows. Balloons, balls, and large toys can easily block the driver's vision.

6. Lock Doors

My Packing List...

216

Travel Awards

Copy onto colored cardstock (or white — and then color them).

Laminate or use clear plastic shelf paper.

Before you leave, make up several awards for special behavior. Give one to each child when he or she exhibits that specific behavior (e.g., best cooperator, special sharer, said a nice thing, helped with baby sister).

What To Take In Your Car

Travel By Car

Digital clock

Map

Wet wipes

Tissues

Spray bottle

Brush and comb

Water bottles (1 for each kid)

Healthy snacks (granola bars or fruit)

Games

Pens, crayons

Paper

Coloring

Tapes or CDs

Make sure you also have a first aid kit and a small litterbag.

Travel By Plane

Traveling by plane can be made easier with a few extra helps.

Gum and candy (for popping ears)

Playing cards

Carry-on bag with games

Car Seat Organizer

Materials Needed:
1 1/2" elastic
Plastic for pockets (optional)
Heavy material (denim or canvas)

For bench seat, measure width of seat and attach
top elastics A and B only.

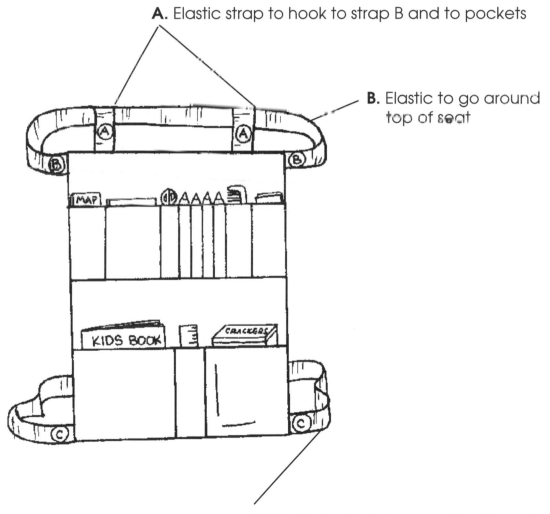

A. Elastic strap to hook to strap B and to pockets

B. Elastic to go around top of seat

C. Elastic to stretch around bottom of seat

Tacklebox Organizer

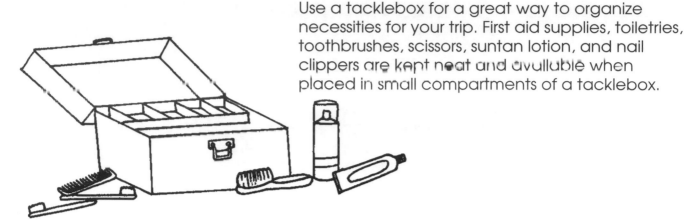

Use a tacklebox for a great way to organize necessities for your trip. First aid supplies, toiletries, toothbrushes, scissors, suntan lotion, and nail clippers are kept neat and available when placed in small compartments of a tacklebox.

Pizza Box

Small pizza boxes are a great way to store car games. They don't take much room, are very sturdy, and close tightly. Decorate and label the top, then cover with clear plastic shelf paper.

Map, Markers, & Stickers

Kids love to help navigate! With colored pen, mark out your travel plans on map. Put little stickers on significant places and let children keep the map. This will help children know where they are and where they are going. Use the full map of the United States found in this chapter.

Nickel Game

Give each child a roll of nickels. Let them know before you start your trip that any time a child says an unkind thing or behaves in an inappropriate way, that child will have to give mom or dad one nickel back. The nickels that children have left upon reaching the destination are theirs to spend.

Lap Boards

For an almost instant lap board, simply glue Velcro® to 3 sides of a 12"x18" piece of hardboard, then glue opposite side of Velcro to pillow case to match hardboard. Or hot-glue small travel pillow directly onto hardboard.

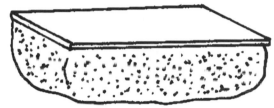

Clip Boards

To make your own clip board, hot glue a large clip or clothespin to hardboard.

Personalize by stenciling or painting as desired.

Purchase girl's hair clips and hot-glue to hardboard for a cute clip board.

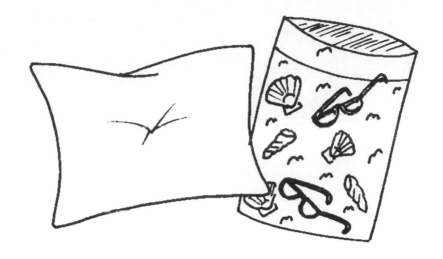

Travel Pillow

Find some material to make a fun pillowcase for your pillows. If you're going to the beach, get fabric with shells or boats. If you're going to the mountains, find fabric with birds, trees, or camouflage.

Travel Bag

Get a small bag or box and decorate for each child. Fill with several small items which are wrapped. Let a child pick one present to open every hour or every 100 miles. When the child has opened all items, he knows he is nearly at his destination. He then has a nice travel bag in which to store keepsakes from his trip.

Ideas for little gifts:

Cute pencils, cars, coloring book, cards, covered cup, sunglasses, clipboard, small games, snacks.

Flannel Board Stories

To keep the memory of a family vacation alive, make a flannel board story. Use the following ideas for a summer or winter vacation story. Copy pictures, cut out, color, laminate, then glue flannel onto back of pictures, or make your own personalized story using travel brochures and photos. Cut out pictures of interesting places. Glue onto cardstock, then glue a piece of flannel onto back of picture.

umbrella

pail

Boat

palm tree

ball

sand castle

fish

shells

Sunshine

crab

sunglasses

Travel Tic-Tac-Toe

Tic-tac-toe is a fun game for everyone. Make a tic-tac-toe travel game by covering the inside of a file folder with felt in the shape of a tic-tac-toe board, then use a marker or black felt for lines. Cut out shapes in felt to use as your markers. Keep a sealable plastic bag inside the folder to store the markers in. Some clever ideas with a traveling theme, instead of Xs and Os, can be found on the next page!

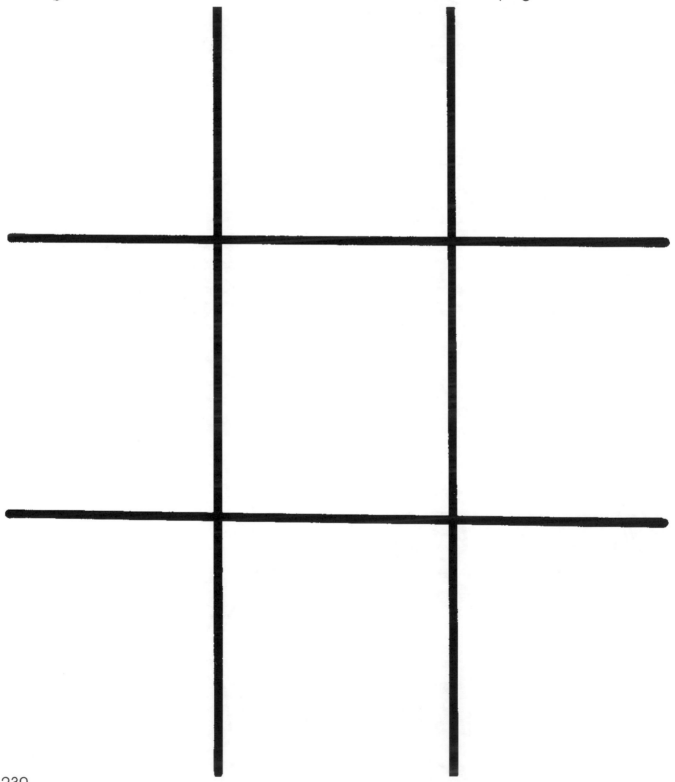

• Make 5 of each desired shape out of felt.

16. Travel Bingo

Copy the Bingo card grid on the next page several times. Copy the pictures below, cut them out, and paste in Bingo grid sheet so all Bingo cards contain the pictures in a different order under each letter. Let kids color, then laminate or use clear plastic shelf paper to protect. Use stickers for markers when playing the game. These are all reusable.

Here is another idea for creating Bingo cards and markers: Glue magnet strips onto the back of the Bingo cards before laminating. Then laminate both the front and back of the cards and use small round magnets as markers. Both the magnet strips and small, round magnets can be purchased at craft stores. This way, there won't be any peeled-off stickers to worry about! Simply store the magnets in a sealable plastic bag.

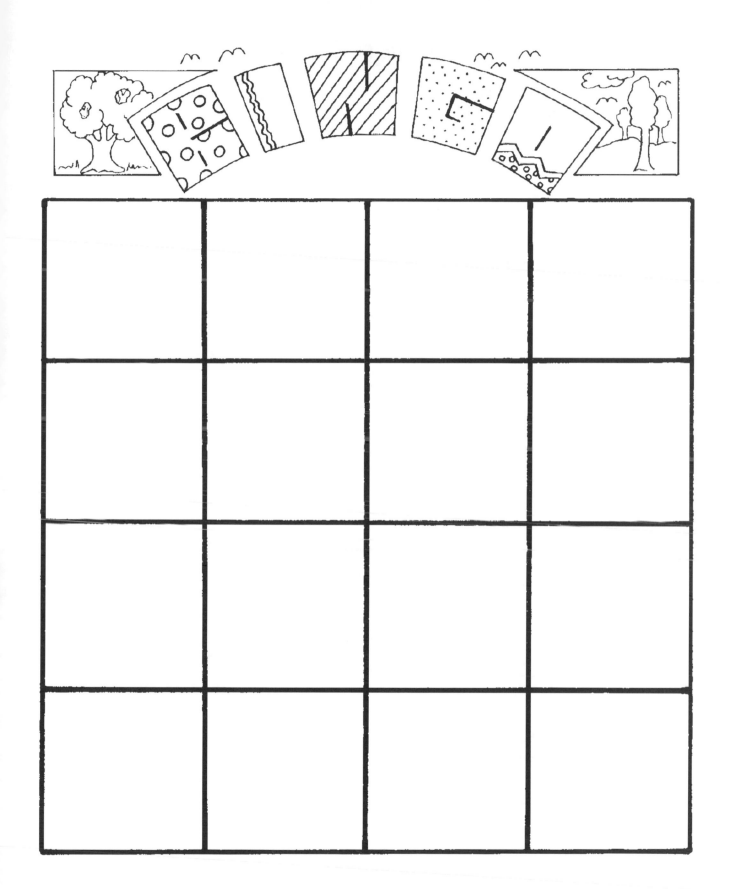

Shape-It-Up Picture Game

Get a sturdy shirt box or pizza box and line top with light-colored felt. Fill the box with all sorts of shapes cut from felt. Kids can create their own pictures. Use the shapes below or cut your own of any size or shape.

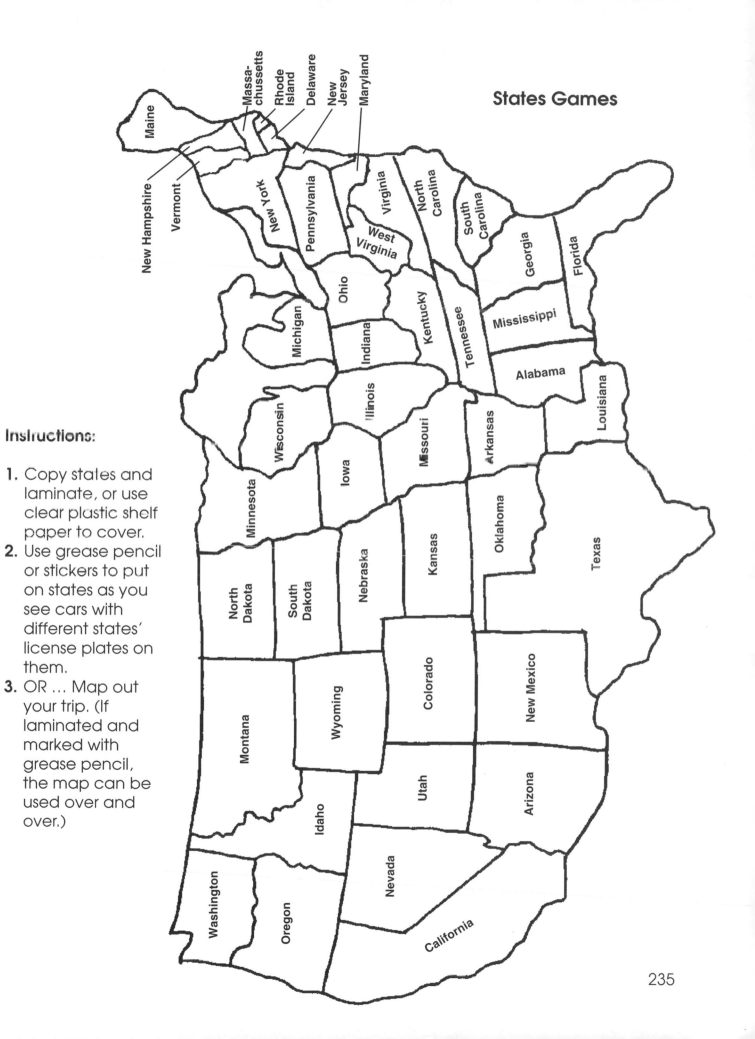

States Games

Instructions:

1. Copy states and laminate, or use clear plastic shelf paper to cover.
2. Use grease pencil or stickers to put on states as you see cars with different states' license plates on them.
3. OR ... Map out your trip. (If laminated and marked with grease pencil, the map can be used over and over.)

Tapes & CDs

Tapes or CDs are often a good distraction. There are a wide variety of choices available. Try educational and informational tapes, children's songs and fingerplays, or some interesting music from an area you are visiting.

Books

Try checking out books from your library about the places you will visit. There are books on airplanes, cars, trains, islands, countries, history, art, or food. Learning is often a lot more fun when it is discovered firsthand. Reading books while visiting an area is not only fun, but very educational.

You can often find coloring books about specific states or countries, too!

Car Games

- Look for five cars of the same color.

- Pick five colors. Find one car of each color.

- Count how many different colored cars you can see in ten minutes.

- Pick an object far ahead of you. Everyone guess how long it will take to reach it. Time the distance.

- Write a long word down on the top of a piece of paper. See how many smaller words you can make out of that one single word.

- Find the letters of the alphabet on license plates (or anywhere). Start with A and try to get through the whole alphabet. Then try doing it backwards!

- Try switching seats periodically. Each seat gives a slightly different view. Let children take turns sitting in front for a specific period of time.

- Pick a type of car and see how many you can spot in a specific period of time.

- See how many different license plates you can spot. Copy the states map in this section and mark off each state with a sticker.

- Try to find numbers on license plates. Start with 1 and see how high you can go.

- **Round Robin Stories:**
  One person starts to tell a story. After 1 minute, he stops. The next person picks up where he left off and continues the story for another minute. Continue on for several minutes, including everyone in the car several times.

- **Twenty Questions:**
  One person picks an object. The others take turns asking questions that require a "yes" or "no" answer. Try to discover the object within 20 questions.

Order Form

QTY.	TITLE	PRICE	CAN. PRICE	SHPG./ HDLG.	TOTAL
	The Complete Book on Kids	$ 24.95	32.95	4.50	
	50 Secrets Your Grocer Doesn't Want You To Know	5.95	7.95	2.00	
	25 Things You Can Do To Feel Even Better Right Now	10.95	13.95	2.00	
	Subtotal				
	Sales Tax (WA residents only, add 8%)				
	Total Enclosed				

Telephone Orders:
Call 1-800-773-3770.
Have your Mastercard
or VISA ready.

Fax Orders:
1-206-820-1836.
Fill out Order Form
and fax.

Postal Orders:
Andante Publishing
PO Box 507
Redmond, WA 98073

Payment:
Please Check One.

☐ Check

☐ *VISA*

☐ MasterCard

Exp. Date _____

Card Number_____

Name on Card_____

_____
NAME

_____
ADDRESS

_____
CITY   STATE   ZIP

_____
DAYTIME PHONE

Quantity discounts available, **1-206-672-8597**

I understand that I may return any books for a full refund if not satisfied.